JOHN GRAY

How to Live for Change and Change for Life

HOW TO CHANGE YOUR LIFE FOR LASTING LOVE, INCREASED SUCCESS AND VIBRANT HEALTH

D1079328

VERMILION
LONDON

13 5 7 9 10 8 6 4 2

Copyright © 2000 by Mars Productions, Inc.

First published in the US by HarperCollins 2000
This edition published in the United Kingdom in 2001 by Vermilion,
an imprint of Ebury Press
The Random House Group Ltd.
Random House
20 Vauxhall Bridge Road
London SW1V 2SA

Random House Australia (Pty) Limited
20 Alfred Street, Milsons Point, Sydney,
New South Wales 2061, Australia

Random House New Zealand Limited
18 Poland Road, Glenfield,
Auckland 10, New Zealand

Random House South Africa (Pty) Limited
Endulini, 5A Jubilee Road, Parktown 2193, South Africa

The Random House Group Limited Reg. No. 954009
www.randomhouse.co.uk

A CIP catalogue record for this book is available from the British Library.

ISBN: 0 09 188226 5

Printed and bound in Great Britain by
Bookmarque Ltd, Croydon, Surrey

For further information about John Gray videos and audio tapes:
Personal Growth Productions
PO Box 51281
Phoenix, AZ 85076- 51281
Telephone: (US) 001-888-627-7836

This book is dedicated to the memory of my mother, Virginia Gray. Her humility, strength, selflessness, and love expressed as a mother to her family and to the many thousands who visited her bookstore, the Aquarian Age Bookshelf, will never be forgotten. Her gentle, youthful, and radiant spirit lives on in me and in all who were lucky enough to know her. She has been my spiritual role model, and I hope this book does justice to the many blessings she has given me.

Thanks, Mom, for always being there, and for staying around to continue helping me.

ACKNOWLEDGMENTS

I thank my wife, Bonnie, and our three daughters, Shannon, Juliet and Lauren, for their continuous love and support. Without their contributions, this book could not have been written.

I thank Jane Friedman at HarperCollins for believing in this book. I thank my editor, Diane Reverand, for her brilliant feedback and advice. I also thank my publicist, Laura Leonard; Matthew Guma for his editorial support; Anne Gaudinier, Rick Harris, and Susan Stone of HarperAudio; and the other incredible staff of HarperCollins.

I thank Linda Michaels, my international agent, for getting my books published in more than fifty languages. I thank Monique Mallory at Planned Television Arts for her hard work in organizing my busy media schedule.

I thank my staff: Steve Grumer, Helen Drake, Bart and Merril Berens, Pollyanna Jacobs, Ian and Ellen Coren, Donna Doiron, Michael Najarian, Sandra Weinstein, Jon Myers, Martin and Josie Brown, Matt Jacobs, Bob Beaudry, and Ronda Coallier for their consistent support and hard work.

I thank my many friends and family members for their support and helpful suggestions: Robert Gray, Virginia Gray,

Robert and Karen Josephson, Clifford McGuire, Jim Kennedy, Alan Garber, Oprah Winfrey, Merv Griffin, Renee Swisco, Paul Goodberg, Darren Stephens and Jackie Tallentyre, Bill Galt, Gail Weaver, Cheryl Lingvall, Dr. Zhi Gang Sha, Dr. Mohsen Hourmanesh, Dr. Ellen Cutler, Jon Carlson, Ramy El Batrawi, and Malcolm Johns.

I thank the hundreds of workshop facilitators who teach Mars-Venus workshops throughout the world and the thousands of individuals and couples who have participated in these workshops. I also thank the Mars-Venus counselors who continue to support my work in their counseling practices.

I thank my parents, Virginia and David Gray, for all their love and support. Though they are no longer here, their love continues to support me. And thanks to Lucile Brixey, who has always been like a second mother to guide and love me.

A special thanks to Anupati Kaleshwar, whose wisdom and experience assisted me greatly in developing a practical understanding of natural healing energy.

I give thanks to God for the incredible energy, clarity, and support I received in bringing forth this book.

CONTENTS

INTRODUCTION

For many people, the beginning of each new year is filled with resolutions, which, after a few weeks, get abandoned. How many times have your best intentions failed?

Although we are inspired to make a positive change, we soon lose our motivation and relapse into old habits. Life goes on the way it did before. After a while, we lose our enthusiasm and faith in ourselves and in others. When the urge to make a change occurs, we discount or dismiss it because we do not trust in our ability to follow through.

One of the first secrets of change is to recognize and trust our ability to make a change and to sustain it. If we do not believe, then we cannot even attempt to change and will not discover our new abilities to create miracles. Then, on this basis of belief, by understanding how miracles occur, we can immediately begin to use our inner potential and create the changes we seek.

**To create change, we must trust in our
ability to follow through and behave
as if miracles are really possible.**

In all my workshops on success, procrastination ranks highest on the list of blocks that hold people back. They want to make a change, but somehow just can't do it. After taking a few steps forward, they are gripped by some mysterious force that restrains them. They are stuck in emotional quicksand. The more they struggle and try to change, the more deeply mired they become. Almost everyone can relate to this in some way. Unless we first learn how change is possible, we will continue to struggle silently or give up on making significant changes altogether.

All life is dynamic and requires change, and life today is so much faster than ever before. Without a new and better understanding of how to make changes, we are doomed to suffer even more. On the brighter side, by applying a few new principles for making a change, life can genuinely be easier. Suddenly, instead of struggling and suffering, we find ourselves effortlessly flowing through life, making the necessary adjustments not just to cope but to make our dreams come true. Instead of trying to row the boat upstream, we joyfully move with the current.

So many times in our relationships we quietly resolve to be more loving. Then our partner says or does one thing, and we are faced once again with a list of reasons why we don't want to try again or open up. Although we may love our partner, we no longer deeply feel that love. Most couples begin by wanting to share a lifetime of passion, then later they really don't understand what happened to take it away. While some are happy to settle for a more traditional loyal but passionless love, most are not, and so dissatisfaction and divorce has increased.

**Most couples start out wanting to share a lifetime
of passion and later really don't understand
what happened to take it away.**

In our business life, we resolve to be more efficient and move ahead in areas where we have procrastinated, only to backslide once again. When we are successful, we earn more money but still find ourselves in greater debt or more stressed so that we cannot enjoy the abundance we have created. Too many families are torn apart by the stresses and pressures of keeping it all together or doing it all. The simple life of a few changes a day is over. Business is now done at the speed of light, and if you can't keep up, then you miss out.

This stress takes its toll not only on our relationships but on our bodies as well. While occasional junk food is fine, to depend on it makes us sick. We resolve to eat healthier food and exercise, and within a few weeks we are back to our same old convenient habits. In the West, we have more divorce, more debt, and more obesity than ever before.

Although medicine has made miraculous advances, people are more dependent on drugs and doctors than ever before. If they are not troubled by extra weight, they are consumed with addictive behaviors like heavy drinking and overworking, or they suffer from allergies and chronic physical pain. In America, the three biggest problems have been increasing debt, domestic violence, and the rising cost of health care. These are the symptoms of our inability to change with the times.

**In relationships we accumulate baggage,
in business we accumulate debt,
and in our bodies we accumulate fat and disease.**

To different degrees, when childhood is over, we become caught in the momentum of our lives and little real or lasting change occurs. Unless this direction is changed, eventually it may lead to physical pain or sickness, decreasing success or the loss of passion in our relationships. To change this direction is what I call a *practical miracle*.

This kind of shift seems like a miracle because, in the past, to make real and lasting changes was nearly impossible. Fortunately, times have changed. Increasing success, lasting love, and vibrant health are practical miracles within the reach of everyone.

I began to realize miracles are real and possible when I personally witnessed several physical healings that modern medicine could not explain. People who were dying of cancer and unable to heal through modern methods were miraculously able to recover and become healthy again.

These kinds of miracles have occurred throughout history and are well documented. Yet, the idea of miracle healings is often dismissed simply because science cannot explain it or it is not easy to repeat in order to study. Simply because we cannot explain miracles doesn't mean that they don't occur. Just because in the past they couldn't be controlled or understood, it doesn't mean that we can't understand them today or, better yet, learn how to create them in our own lives.

When I witnessed many of these healings and then directly experienced a miraculous physical healing of the blindness in my left eye, my mind suddenly opened to the reality that miracles are real. They have occurred throughout history and are happening today. They occur not only in the area of health but in all areas of life.

In my search to understand and explain how miracles occur, I discovered that the same principles that create a physical healing can increase success and create more loving relationships. I also learned that miracles can occur even when our problems are not enormous or life-threatening.

By understanding how miracle healings take place, it becomes easy to understand how miracles can happen in all areas of our lives.

Miracles occur all the time but we normally just call it luck. Attributing our success to luck, however, implies that we have no control over the good fortune we experience. The truth is, there are reasons why good things happen. Choices are made and the results come. When good results come and we don't know how we did it, then we call it luck. We call it luck only because we don't clearly understand how our beliefs, feelings, thoughts, attitudes, choices, and actions determine all the results we get in life.

Through learning the way people think, feel, and so on, prior to a miracle or "lucky event," we can learn how to start creating practical miracles in our own lives. Throughout *How to Live for Change and Change for Life* we will explore and understand nine guiding principles that, when observed, can assist us in creating the results we want in life. Good fortune will not be left up to luck or destiny but can be something we consciously generate each day.

The Placebo Effect

Often, when miracles occur, people attribute the good fortune to strong faith or to the power of suggestion. There is an incredible power in believing. However, positive belief or optimism is not enough by itself. It is only one of the nine principles for creating practical miracles.

When a miracle healing takes place, sometimes, after a few weeks, the relief or healing disappears and the unhealthy symptoms come back. As a result, doctors and scientists are often wary of sudden, miraculous cures. While they recognize that such cures do occur, they feel that, in the majority of cases, the advancement is temporary and that the condition has not been truly healed.

Rather than wonder, "Does miraculous healing really occur?" we would do better to ask, "How and why does faith heal and why is it sometimes temporary?"

Then we can ask, "What can be done so that illness or problems don't return?"

Once we understand the nine principles of creating miracles, it will become clear why these cures occur, why they go away, and how to make the healing permanent. With this insight we can learn how to stay healthy and avoid sickness and pain in the first place.

The temporary nature of miracle healings, transformations, or changes is well documented in science. It is called the placebo effect. Often patients will get better simply because they believe they will. Studies repeatedly show that some people improve even when given a simple sugar pill containing absolutely no medicine or active ingredient. The sheer belief that they are being treated for their problem or condition creates temporary healing.

The placebo effect appears in other situations as well. People will listen to a motivational speaker or preacher and suddenly be inspired to make positive changes to increase success or love more fully. Although they leave feeling revved up, they soon regress and aren't able to follow through with the change.

It is not unusual for people who order exercise equipment after watching a late-night infomercial to rarely use their products after a few weeks. Many never even open the box. What equipment do you have around the house that you are not using?

For most of us, enthusiasm fades fast. While some people continue ordering the next quick fix, others are quick to mistrust or dismiss miraculous claims. Anything that promises a quick fix or creates miraculous change is often viewed as a fad or gimmick that really doesn't work. As with any other placebo, if we believe, the miracle will begin . . . but belief is not enough to sustain it.

When change is not sustained, many people become jaded and stop believing.

Many people experience the placebo effect in matters of love. When they first meet someone, they are overcome with emotion. Then, within a few weeks to a few years, they grow disappointed. In one minute they fall in love, and then later fall out of love. A few such experiences from their perspective or from their lover's cause them to mistrust their own feelings of love or the attention and affection of others.

When we are certain we have found the person of our dreams, we fall in love. First we believe they are the one, and then we fall in love. Falling in love occurs when our hearts are open to the possibility that at last we have gotten what we are looking for. Once we get to know the person and we stop believing they are the one for us, then we fall out of love.

Ironically, when we fall in love it is often with someone we don't even know or with whom we have had very little interaction. But if we believe they may be the one, we will react as if we truly have found the right person for us. Abruptly all our loneliness and pain disappears, at least for a while. This is why falling in love can be such a relief. It also explains why falling out of love can be such a letdown. When we stop believing our partner is the one, all our past unresolved pain that was relieved by falling in love suddenly returns.

The problem with believing and being repeatedly disappointed is that we stop believing we can get what we need and that we can make our dreams come true. As a result, life becomes boring and loses its sparkle and shine. We become stuck and frequently accept our lifelessness as a natural symptom of growing old. Fortunately, it is not.

To create and enjoy lasting love, increasing success, and vibrant health, we must continue to believe. Yet, we must also recognize that believing that miracles are possible is only one of the many principles required to create and sustain practical changes in our lives. Without an understanding of the other required principles, then we stop believing in the power of believing.

When we stop believing in the possibility of positive change, then we have no power to change. With a new awareness of the other factors that allow believing to create sustained results, we are then set free to believe once again. We can easily see what was missing before and we can now begin filling in the missing pieces so that our desires to change can be sustained. With this shift, we are free once again to experience the power and wonder that come from opening our minds and hearts to the real possibilities of change and transformation.

The problem with belief alone is that, after being repeatedly let down, we stop believing.

Optimism is the basis of lasting inspiration. Change can only begin and then be sustained if we continue to believe. Without hope, we have no motivation. Without hope, we will never plant the seeds of our success, settling instead for what we already have. We resign ourselves to the limited belief that this is as good as it gets. While there is a certain comfort in this acceptance, there is no passion, and there are no miracles.

The Limits of Natural Law

Developing the power to create practical miracles doesn't mean that you can do anything or cause anything to happen. Science teaches us that everything in the universe follows certain natural laws. At the same time, science also admits that it doesn't *fully* understand the natural laws that govern everything around us. But, just because more is possible, it doesn't mean that anything is possible.

For example, you cannot heal a broken bone in a day, but, if someone is not healing, you can stimulate and awaken his or her own natural self-healing ability. As a result, the bone will begin healing in the same way it would heal in a healthier person.

How to Live for Change and Change for Life explains the governing principles responsible for changing your life in all areas through updating your beliefs, feelings, thoughts, attitudes, and so on. By changing your inner world, you can then more effectively influence the outer world, your relationships, and your body.

Even with miraculous power, you cannot make all relationships work. You cannot please everyone or be pleased by everyone. There are definite limits. You cannot continue to eat poison and remain healthy. You cannot sustain success or personal fulfillment in your career when your soul wants to be doing something else.

On the other hand, you could be in the right relationship and still struggle, because you are not using your miraculous potential to create lasting love. You could be in the right career and still fail to succeed only because you are not using your miraculous power to increase success. You could be eating healthy foods and doing other good things for your body and spirit, but if you are not using your miraculous power to create vibrant health, you may still get sick.

Why Some People Heal and Others Don't

Every doctor or healer at some time is frustrated because what has worked for others does not work all the time or with every patient. *How to Live for Change and Change for Life* answers the question many doctors, counselors, and healers ask: "Why do some people heal while others do not?" With these new insights, it all becomes clear. As a result, one can easily begin to see how the patient or client is not using his or her potential for success, love, and health.

**Every doctor or healer at some time
is frustrated because what has worked for others
does not work all the time.**

Although it is naive to think anything is possible, a healthy belief regarding miracles is to admit that we really don't ever know for sure what is possible and what is not. One thing I know for sure, from this study of miracles, is that much more than we can imagine is possible. But, with this openness to all possibilities, we must also accept that there are limits. We are open to possibilities but we are confident about only what we have directly experienced.

The truth is, everything we observe is miraculous, from the latest technological advances to the extravagant bounty of apples that grow from a single seed. When your finger is cut and the body begins healing itself, it is a miracle. Yet, as soon as these miracles become common to our experience, we stop seeing them as miracles. The changes you experience through using the nine techniques for creating practical miracles will at first seem miraculous, but, eventually, as you get used to your new power, it very quickly will feel normal and natural.

Poison Is Still Poison

Miraculous powers can't make poisonous, unhealthy food good for you. Poison is still poison, but you can wean yourself from its influence. Through healing your sickness, you are then free to pursue what is good for you. With healing comes the wisdom of knowing what is right for you and having the correct motivation to make the change.

When you have healed the cause of a condition, the desire for unhealthy foods or situations diminishes. In a similar but opposite manner, when you ingest something that is not good for you, without healing, your craving to repeat that activity increases. Without learning how to create practical miracles, people become stuck for many years hopelessly attempting to change bad habits.

Without learning how to create practical miracles, we struggle for years trying to change bad habits.

We do not have the power to change the intrinsic value of something, but we do have the power to change what we desire. If you desire poison and are under the influence of an unhealthy craving, compulsion, or addiction, it is a practical miracle to change this desire. More accurately stated, you have the power to release yourself from the grasp of these unhealthy or false desires and reconnect with natural and healthy ones.

One of the greatest practical miracles I have experienced personally is the ability to release unhealthy craving, compulsions, and addictive tendencies. When you develop this power, life becomes so much easier and is so much more satisfying.

For example, if you have spent your life not liking salad,

it is quite a miracle not only to hunger for it but also to enjoy it with excitement and delight. If you have spent your life getting upset or feeling hurt when you didn't get what you wanted, it is wonderful to release this compulsive tendency that demands life be perfect.

As you will discover throughout *How to Live for Change and Change for Life*, this new millennium is a time of accelerated change. By opening your awareness to the new possibilities that exist, you can begin making changes that you didn't think were possible. With a new awareness of the nine principles for creating practical miracles along with new practical tools and techniques, you will begin to realize this new potential. It is within the reach of every person to take charge of his or her personal destiny and, regardless of past mistakes or limitations, begin today creating lasting love, increasing success, and vibrant health.

John Gray
MAY 3, 2000

1

PRACTICAL MIRACLES
FOR MARS AND VENUS

Walking on water is certainly miraculous, but walking peacefully on earth is an even greater miracle. Changing water to wine is wondrous, but it is more practical to change an unhealthy craving into a healthy desire. Raising the dead is clearly a miraculous demonstration of God's power, but so is healing your daughter's tummyache or removing the pain of an earache or, better yet, feeling vibrantly healthy so you don't get sick in the first place. This power to create practical miracles is now within the reach of every person.

Mankind has long awaited a special time when our capacity to create miracles would occur. All of the great religious leaders and prophets have predicted this time. In the last fifty years, the incredible speed of change triggered by new technologies and television has literally transformed the consciousness of the world. Just as the dawn precedes the rising sun, the last fifty years have glowed in the imminent and radiant light of the rising sun of a new age for mankind.

The dramatic spiritual changes in the West, inspired by the pope and other religious leaders, or the inspirational writings of self-help books that dominate the bestseller lists (and many more that don't make the lists), reflect this increasing awareness of the need for change and the different ways to accomplish change. These changes are not just of a spiritual nature; they have occurred in every segment of secular society as well. The radical social, political, economic, and health changes that have occurred in such a short period of time are historically unprecedented. Never has so much change occurred in such a short time, and never has so much knowledge and information been available to the public.

Not all these changes are necessarily good, but they have been needed to bring into focus what is most excellent or helpful to realize our new potential. Sometimes we need to go left to realize that we really need to go right. Mistakes are a part of the learning curve. Making a change for the worse and clearly recognizing its futility can become the catalyst to create a radical change for the better. Clearly, Adolph Hitler's demonstration of extreme one-way thinking revealed to the world the dangers of believing there is one superior race, one superior way of thinking and behaving. This fundamental shift from one-way thinking to seeing the good in all has unlocked the door for accelerated progress and transformation.

In simple terms, what makes this new age unique is that people now have the potential to experience God's presence and power within their hearts, and, as a result, accelerated change is possible. With this shift, humanity is finally capable of bringing "heaven to earth" and creating a world of peace, love, health, and prosperity for all.

In biblical days, Jesus spoke of a time when people would have the capacity to understand the truth and even surpass the wonders that he worked. He was speaking of our new potential to create practical miracles. Buddha also spoke of a time when mankind would be delivered from the suffering of ignorance. Moses spoke of the Promised Land of milk and honey and the salvation of his people. The great leaders of all faiths, East and West, ancient and new, have predicted an age of universal peace, love, justice, and prosperity. For some, the ancient predictions mean the end of the world as we know it. But for all, it is the beginning of something very special.

This special time is finally here—it is not in five years or twenty years. The shift has already taken place. To appreciate this change, we just have to begin using our new potential. Humanity has been preparing for this change for thousands of years. This shift is similar to the ripening process of a fruit. At a certain time, the pear, which gradually grows and develops over time, is suddenly ripe. You can feel its sweetness by simply reaching up at the right time, and, with a slight twist, it effortlessly comes off. Prior to the moment of ripeness, it is a struggle to pull it off, and when tasted, it is not so tender or sweet.

In a similar manner, what was previously difficult or even unattainable for most is now universally available. This recognition is based not on a psychic vision of the future but on direct experience, a simple observation of what is now happening.

During the past twenty-eight years, besides counseling and teaching about relationships, I have successfully practiced and taught a variety of healing and meditation techniques that enable people to increase their personal fulfillment and outer success. In my workshops today, the immediate results that even beginners experience from healing and meditation practices are light-years ahead of what participants experienced a few years ago. Most participants achieve in one day a level of attainment that in many ways is equal to what took me twenty-five years of disciplined practice to attain.

From Monk to Millionaire

In my twenties, although my fundamental belief was and is Christian, I was a celibate Hindu monk for nine years. My common practice was to spend more than ten hours a day in meditation. I led a very simple life and often ate only one bowl of food a day. As with any devoted endeavor, the more you practice, the better you get. Although I became an expert meditator after about eight years, it took another twenty years of regular practice for my experiences to awaken my inner potential for creating practical miracles. This dedicated effort is no longer necessary. In just a few weeks of easy practice, workshop participants and clients today can achieve many of the positive benefits and results that took me twenty-nine years to experience.

The practical benefits of meditation are not limited to spiritual attainment or peace of mind. Advanced meditation and self-healing practices also can greatly awaken one's potential for success, love, and health. Don't let the word "advanced" scare you from the practices that I will suggest. The advanced techniques are the easiest. The main reason people lose interest in meditation is that they are taught the beginner techniques. As a result, it is boring, tedious, and difficult. When you learn the advanced techniques, it suddenly becomes interesting and fun, and you experience real results.

As a student of karate at nine years old, I had the good fortune to have a master teacher who broke away from the ancient teachings of first learning all the beginning moves. We immediately went to the advanced moves, which were stimulating, held my interest, and were appropriate. People in the past needed the beginning exercises, but today we don't.

This is also similar to learning the piano. A young child needs all the beginning moves and exercises. At age forty-five, I decided that I wanted to learn to play the piano. I found a teacher who was willing to skip all the beginner's practice and teach me advanced moves. Within a week, I was playing my favorite songs from *Les Misérables*. The whole process held my interest, and within six months I could play twenty of my favorite songs.

Because you are already advanced but just don't know it, by learning the advanced meditation techniques, you will experience immediately the benefits that in the past may have taken a lifetime to achieve. Of course, there are many other factors that create success, but I attribute my success as a teacher and writer to my own personal mastery of meditation and prayer. The most important transformational skill I have learned in my thirty years of research has been the regular practice of meditation and prayer. To sustain success at work while nurturing a loving family and a healthy, fit body requires tremendous spiritual grounding and experience. Since I made spirituality my first priority, the rest of my life has flourished.

To be financially successful, nurture a loving family, and sustain a healthy, fit body requires tremendous spiritual grounding.

In my journey, I have literally followed the message of Jesus: "Seek ye first the kingdom of heaven, and all else will be given unto you." By finding my connection to God within myself, I was able to access tremendous creative power for change. This simple message is the basis of creating practical miracles. The same message is mentioned in all religions, but now is the time when its inherent truth is available to all in a practical sense.

In the famous Christian "Lord's Prayer," Jesus teaches his students to say to God, "Let thy kingdom come." He implies that it is not necessary to postpone the experience of heaven until we die. We can bring it now into our daily experience. John the Baptist also heralds the message of Jesus by proclaiming to his people that "the kingdom of heaven is at hand." Though these messages gave hope to the people, Jesus clearly taught his people that they were not fully ready to understand his teachings but that one day they would, and then they, too, would do miracles.

Since that time has come, the spiritual and practical powers that were previously only attainable by a select few are suddenly easy to attain. In the past, you needed to pull away from life and make many sacrifices to attain even a glimpse of real spiritual love and power. Now, all it takes is a good teacher and the application of new skills and principles appropriate to this new age of miracles.

Witnessing Practical Miracles

I began realizing that miracles were truly possible when I both experienced and witnessed healing and the recovery from sickness. When patients were given up to die, I witnessed miraculous cures provided by lifestyle changes, alternative medicine, and dietary changes. Most amazing or miraculous to me were the benefits gained from getting an "energy healing" or "spiritual healing." After seeing this with my own eyes, I began to realize that miracles happen all the time in all areas of life. Now, in retrospect, I see every kind of healing, whether it is from a heart transplant, acupuncture, a dietary shift, or a spiritual healer as a miracle. Miracles come in different ways and affect our lives in different ways.

A miracle is not just a physical cure. A miracle could be a physical healing, or it could mean that an emotional block disappears, and one suddenly experiences a stronger ability to feel love for others or themselves. For others with pain or sickness, their miracles are a healing from physical pain. During an energy healing session, chronic pain often simply disappears and never returns.

For others, a healing means the sudden motivation and

ability to make a few healthy dietary changes and then lose extra weight. As a result, their bodies eventually get better, and their pain gradually goes away. A practical miracle generally frees people from whatever is holding them back from being more loving, successful, and healthy. This process unfolds in gradual stages. All problems are not magically solved by a miracle, but the blocks that hold us back from solving our problems responsibly can begin to disappear one at a time and one day at a time.

The days of struggling for years with bad habits or limiting patterns are over. This does not mean people can now do without doctors, counselors, nutritionists, and other professionals. The natural energy healing that comes from exercising your power to create practical miracles works together with good medicine, nutrition, and lifestyle. Natural energy healing enhances the effectiveness of whatever treatment you are using or may need to use.

I know this is hard to believe. It is still amazing to me. In my experience of teaching workshops during the past thirty years, this kind of rapid healing did not occur. There were occasional reports of miraculous change, but not for everyone. Certainly, almost all of those who were healed felt inspired, happier, and motivated, but in many cases the results didn't last. The high that came from spending many days together focusing on growth was quickly followed by a low. Too often those who crashed would blame themselves and become disillusioned with their own personal potential.

Although the experience of new love and power was real, after a few months many of the insights and healing experiences faded, like a dream upon awakening. When I recognized this, I stopped teaching long transformational workshops to focus on short ones and on seminars that conveyed immediately such useful and effective information as the ideas contained in *Men Are from Mars, Women Are from Venus*.

Healing Blindness

In 1993, as my success in life was rising dramatically to a new level, and my dreams of helping the world were coming true, I experienced an eye infection. While vacationing in another country, I had unknowingly ingested from my food particular parasites that attack the eyes and cause blindness. Within a few months, I became legally blind in my left eye. As the vision in my eye dimmed, my life became very gloomy. On rainy days or dark evenings, I could not even drive safely. To raise my spirits, I reminded myself that this was another challenge, and that by facing it, there would eventually be a gift. Every other unexpected setback in my life had in time redirected me and brought me some new strength. Ultimately, my blindness would do the same.

I sought help from the world's leading eye experts. During a frustrating six-month process, I was examined and diagnosed by more than sixteen experts. Unfortunately, there was little they could do. The condition got progressively worse.

After struggling against depression by using my tools of emotional processing, I gradually reached a greater degree of peace and acceptance. At the same time, I was still motivated to find a cure. Meanwhile, I made a lifestyle change and decided to stop working as hard and start doing what I wanted to do in life.

Natural Healing

At the time, my then new book, *Men Are from Mars, Women Are from Venus*, had been doing well, so I rewarded myself with a new, beautiful, fast car. Though this may not sound like a big change to a lot of people, it was for me. I was used to living within my means and didn't own many expensive or flashy things. In addition, my wife and I try to be respectful of the environment, and the car I wanted was a gas-guzzler.

My wife was surprised when I mentioned that I was going to go out to buy this car. I explained to her that it was what I wanted, and we could afford it, so I was doing it. When I told her that it was a black car, she replied, "Black is not a good car color; you'll have to wash it every week. And I know you don't want to do that."

My immediate response was, "That's okay. I want a dirty, black, fast car."

Within a week after I bought the car, we went on a week-long driving tour through northern California to Oregon and back. We breathed fresh air, walked through forests, swam in lakes, meditated in the fresh mountain air, and slept as late as we wished. I drove free and fast on wide expansive highways surrounded by panoramic views. This heavenly experience distracted me from the stress in my life and from my eye condition. I had fretted enough. It was time to get on with my life. After five days on the road, I started noticing that the air seemed so much cleaner. Then I realized that the vision in my left eye was no longer a blur and had started to sharpen.

It was a miracle. By the time we got home, much of my vision had returned. By following my heart and connecting with nature in a relaxed, peaceful, and happy manner, my body's natural self-healing capacity was awakened. It was a spontaneous healing.

Yet, this healing did not happen just by chance or good fortune. There were clear and definite reasons that it occurred. I later came to realize how important doing what you want in life and spending time in nature are for self-healing to occur. By taking that trip and doing the things we enjoyed, I was giving myself the elements I was missing in my life so that my body's natural healing power could be awakened in my eyes. Though many other elements are also necessary for vibrant health, for me personally the ingredients my body needed to heal itself were experienced on that trip, allowing the practical miracle of healing to occur.

Ultimately, we all have a wide range of important needs. When we don't meet them, we get sick, our relationships suffer, or our business success is limited. Lacking only one of our many needs may cause us to stall, failing to move ahead. When we consciously or inadvertently meet those needs, then spontaneous healing or a miracle occurs.

When we struggle to find a cure or solution to a problem and it is not working, we are most often looking in the wrong direction. When a room is dark, you don't have to fight the darkness or develop special glasses to see in the dark. Instead, if you simply switch on the light, the darkness disappears. This is the way miracles work.

When you bring in what you are missing, then what you are wanting spontaneously occurs and the problem just disappears. The gardener does nothing to grow a seed into a tree. Mother Nature does it. Within the seed is the perfect blueprint of the tree. Working in harmony with nature, the gardener provides the right soil, water, fresh air, and sunshine. Automatically nature can work its miracles and a little tiny seed eventually grows into a great tree. Without the help of the gardener, that little seed would remain a seed in a bag, patiently waiting to be planted. Practical miracles occur when we work together with nature to produce a specific result.

What distinguishes a practical miracle from what is commonly understood as a miracle is not only the practical benefit it provides but also the way it is created. Traditionally miracles were considered to be for the lucky and fortunate. People who experienced them just assumed they were lucky, and others who didn't experience miracles mistakenly assumed that they were just not lucky. Even worse, when a person doesn't get a miraculous healing, he might mistakenly conclude that he is somehow unworthy of healing or that God is punishing him for his past mistakes.

Practical miracles dispel this myth and open the door to understanding logically the definite conditions that allow for a specific miracle to occur. Miracles don't just happen for some and not for others. They occur when specific conditions are nurtured. Like a seed, with the right minerals, water, air, and sunshine, anyone, no matter who you are or what you have done in the past, can begin creating practical miracles.

2

___

RECOGNIZING OUR
NEW POTENTIAL

With the birth of the twenty-first century, mankind has taken a giant leap. It is as though a veil has suddenly been lifted and what was difficult before suddenly has become very easy. The ability to create accelerated change is suddenly within every person's reach. But, to access and develop this new potential, we must first be aware that it exists. Without this recognition and understanding of our new potential we will not bother to develop it. Throughout this book, you will discover that to develop this potential, you have to begin using it.

The days of seeking our potential are over. It is here. History is filled with attempts to find the truth and glimpse our potential. Now the time is finally here and our new challenge is to begin using it. It is as though we have been shopping for the right car and now we have it. Our new task is to start it up and begin driving. In the past, the most common soul desire was to find God, but today our soul desire is to bring God into this world.

There is no arduous path of finding our potential. It is right here. To access it we must let go of outdated beliefs and habits of the past. Since the veil has been lifted and our inner potential is now available to us, this task of releasing outdated beliefs and habits can be achieved simply by remembering and behaving as if we have this new power. It is that simple. The nine guiding principles of creating practical miracles will assist you in making this shift. Let these nine principles be the stars you set your compass to when choosing your direction in life. They are:

1. Believe as if miracles are possible (and let your actions and responses reflect this knowing).

2. Live as if you are free to do what you want (and let your actions and responses reflect this new freedom).

3. Learn as if you are a beginner (and let your actions and responses reflect this humility).

4. Love as if for the first time (and let your actions and responses reflect this forgiving attitude).

5. Give as if you already have what you need (and let your actions and responses reflect an attitude of gratitude and generosity).

6. Work as if money doesn't matter (and let your actions and responses always come from choice).

7. Relax as if everything will be okay (and let your actions and responses reflect this trusting attitude).

8. Talk to God as if you are being heard (and recognize how your actions and responses are enriched and empowered whenever you ask for help).

9. Feast as if you can have whatever you want (and let your actions and responses reflect an attitude of abundance).

Building Confidence

The secret for awakening your inner potential is to act and respond to life as if you do have this new potential. If you wait for someone to prove it to you or do it for you, then in that action alone you are disconnecting from your inner potential. Finding this potential literally takes a leap of faith. This leap does not have to be a tremendous risk, although it may feel that way. By gradually following the nine guiding principles and, more important, by practicing the techniques for creating practical miracles, you will create the time to generate new experiences and build confidence.

As you practice the techniques and directly experience your new inner potential, then your belief will increase and your power will manifest. It is a gradual process of increasing confidence, much like learning to ride a bike. Once you gain the confidence, it is effortless.

To achieve greater confidence, new techniques and practical skills are essential. But first we must be aware of, and begin releasing, some of our old beliefs and habits of thinking. Unless some of these limited beliefs are recognized, you will not take the time to read on and begin practicing the easy techniques for creating practical miracles.

As you read through the list of nine guiding principles, you probably experienced many of your old beliefs and habits of thinking beginning to surface. These beliefs are what could hold you back from developing your new potential. Just being aware that these are limiting beliefs helps your new consciousness begin to release them. These are a few examples of common outdated beliefs from the past. Remember: They may have been true in the past, but they are no longer appropriate.

GUIDING PRINCIPLES	LIMITING BELIEFS
1. Believe as if miracles are possible:	Miracles may happen for others but not for me, or miracles may happen occasionally, but not every day. I cannot change.
2. Live as if you are free to do what you want:	But I am not free; I must be careful to do what others think is okay or I will be laughed at or rejected. There is only one right way to behave, and if I want to get ahead I should follow that. I must hide my true self.
3. Learn as if you are a beginner:	I can't learn as if I am a beginner. I am an adult and to be respected I must appear to have all the answers. I don't need any help.
4. Love as if for the first time:	I can't freely love again. I have been hurt before and to protect myself from being hurt again I must guard my heart and hold back unless a person is truly worthy of my love and trust. I don't trust others.
5. Give as if you already have what you need:	I can't give my partner anything more until I get back what I deserve. Unless they give me more, I have nothing left to give. I have run out of love and energy.

GUIDING PRINCIPLES	LIMITING BELIEFS
6. Work as if money doesn't matter:	I am not free to work as if money doesn't matter. I have to work to pay my bills. I couldn't earn enough money working at my ideal job. I cannot do what I would choose to do.
7. Relax as if everything will be okay:	I can't relax. I have real problems that will not go away by ignoring them. There are real reasons why I can't sleep at night and why I feel stressed out during the day. There is nothing I can do to make things better.
8. Talk to God as if you are being heard:	Prayer is for children. I prayed before and nothing happened. People prayed all the way through the Dark Ages and the plague wiped them out. Nobody is listening. If I am to succeed in life, it is up to me. There are no free rides.
9. Feast as if you can have whatever you want:	I can't eat whatever I want. I am already overweight or sick from what I eat. I have to sacrifice and live on a diet if I want to look good and be healthy. I am missing out.

These are just a few examples of the old outdated beliefs by which we live our lives. Take some time to read over the list of nine guiding principles and reflect on your own limiting beliefs that come up. Put each principle at the top of a sheet of paper and then write out all your doubts and questions regarding the practicality of these principles. Then, as you read on, you will pull out of this book the insight to support you in challenging and releasing the particular limited beliefs that hold you back. Gradually as you read this book, go back to your list of objections and challenge them with your new insight and experience.

Remember that your limited beliefs were often true and valid in the past, but today they are not. Your potential has changed and you are now capable of much more. Babies at birth cannot suddenly walk; but, when the right time comes, they start to crawl, and then, eventually, in one day everything changes. In one moment they stand up and begin to walk. When the time is right, it is that simple.

A child is dependent on love to survive, so it often becomes an intelligent coping mechanism for the child to accommodate its parents because the child needs their love. Once we are adults, however, we no longer depend on our parents' support and therefore do not need to accommodate them. We are free to be ourselves.

In a similar way, this common shift reflects the new potential we all now have. In the past, we were dependent on others for the truth, and thus we needed to accommodate and follow others to know what is right; but today we are like new adults capable of knowing what is right within our own hearts. Since we are no longer so dependent on others to know what is true, letting go of limiting beliefs is almost automatic.

The first step is simply to be aware of our outdated beliefs and question their relevance today. By questioning them, we open the door to collect new evidence to support new beliefs. It is this opening that makes the techniques for creating practical miracles work. As you apply the different techniques and follow the nine guiding principles, it works best if you do it with the scientific attitude that you're testing to see what is really true. Give yourself permission to question and doubt, but act as if you do have this new potential. In this way, you will gather experiences so that your belief is based solely on your own experience and not just because someone told you. Prove to yourself that you either have or don't have this new potential.

Let the insights and exercises in *How to Live for Change and Change for Life* support you in overcoming the old beliefs that were given to you first by your parents and society and then confirmed by your own experiences in life. To update your beliefs, give yourself a chance to generate new experiences. By taking a risk and opening your mind and heart by trying something new, you will develop and support new updated beliefs most effectively regarding who you are and what you can accomplish in life.

Creating Heaven on Earth

The time to create a heaven on earth is now. What holds us back are the memories of all the times we wanted more and failed. In the past, when we resolved to make a change and experienced failure or a setback, it was hard to continue on trying to change. This failure then holds us back from trying again. Because of repeated disappointments and dissatisfaction in life, our failures and the failures of others gradually jaded us. We believed and then accepted life's limitations. Though this approach was appropriate in the past, it is now outdated. To let go of the past, we must set a deliberate intention to act as if the beliefs of the past are limited and therefore no longer appropriate or useful to us.

To act as if something is possible is like pretending. Yet, to break free from your beliefs, the first step is to pretend that something else is true and then see if it really is. In this process, it is okay to doubt as long as you go ahead and act as if something is possible. You will certainly risk failure again, but you will also have the possibility of new success. Take the leap. By putting into practice the practical techniques for each of the nine principles, you will be assured of success right away.

A child can be ready to walk, but if he or she doesn't see others walking, it is much more difficult and time consuming to realize this new potential. Without a guide or picture of what it looks like to walk, it is much more difficult to learn. If our only example is other babies crawling around, we may never learn to walk. The nine techniques for creating practical miracles point the way to stand up and manifest your inner potential. Once you get the hang of it, you can forget the techniques and develop your own personal style.

The new possibilities that exist today for men and women to materialize their dreams are truly miraculous. This sudden and complete shift in our potential is as radical as the shift from boiling water to steam or from night to day. On Monday we are poor, and on Tuesday we get an unexpected letter containing a check for one million dollars. The only catch is that we have to read our mail. Unless we open the letter, deposit the check, and begin using the money, we will continue to be poor. To begin utilizing our new potential, we must actively begin to apply a new approach to life

---

**The ability to create the life you have
always wanted is now available.**

All of our current attitudes are based on our old potential. To realize our new potential we must recognize that almost all of our old ways of thinking will hold us back. Although they were effective in the past, they cannot access our new potential. Fortunately, this is not a difficult process. All we need is the awareness of what is available to us and the simple information for how to access it, and suddenly it will come forward and be realized. It is no surprise that the younger generation, which is not burdened as much by old ways of thinking, and is maturing in the age of the Internet, has leaped forward in its ability to make money.

It is time to stop crawling and to stand up and walk. It is time to let go of our old ways of thinking. Our old beliefs are primarily based on our past experiences. By creating new experiences, we can begin to change these limiting beliefs. By just remembering the nine guiding principles and acting as if they were possible, you will be surprised to find out that they are. As you begin experiencing right away your new potential, your limiting beliefs will disappear. With this shift you will open the door to access your power to create practical miracles every day. Because the time is now right, if you try again, no matter how old you are, you can succeed. You can increase success, restore lasting love, and begin creating vibrant health.

3

THE NINE
GUIDING PRINCIPLES

In practical terms, by applying the nine guiding principles you can start making changes in your life that previously seemed impossible for you. Any new skill is easier to learn if we have examples or demonstrations to follow. For easy assimilation of the nine principles, it is helpful to have a vision of possibilities. There are unique benefits that come directly from applying each of the nine guiding principles. While these are some of the benefits, you may experience your own unique benefits and miracles. These are a few examples of changes or practical miracles I have regularly witnessed in my own life and in the lives of participants of my workshops.

1. **Believe as if miracles are possible.** Using this guiding principle, participants have hope again. With hope they are motivated to make new resolutions. Miraculously, they find that they are able to follow through. They feel the confi-

dence to do things they have been putting off for years. Procrastination no longer holds us back when we believe and experience that the miracle of change can really happen.

2. Live as if you are free to do what you want. Using this guiding principle and applying self-healing techniques in a group or with a healer, in ten minutes, chronic pain and other health problems have miraculously disappeared. After a "miracle healing," whether it be physical or emotional, instead of feeling burdened by your lot in life, suddenly you feel your new freedom to be all that you have the potential to be. With this experience, you gain the support to enjoy life, to "live freely" as if no one is holding you back.

"Miracle healings" are not new; they have occurred throughout history. They have been fully documented during the past thousand years in every culture and tradition in the world. Even in the last one hundred years, the scrutiny of the most rigorous scientific research and testing has shown that unexplained immediate recovery from a variety of deadly diseases is a reality.

And miracle healings continue to occur. No educated medical researcher doubts this. The reason some scientists, researchers, and doctors minimize or cringe at the mention of miracle healings is that they can't duplicate or understand them.

Miraculous healing in the past was a hit-or-miss occurrence and thus "nonscientific," simply because people could not explain or replicate it. A few people were healed but most were not. It is important to recognize that just because something can't be understood, it doesn't mean that it didn't happen or doesn't exist.

In my workshops and while studying with healers around the world, I personally have witnessed almost every illness—from such serious diseases and conditions as stage-four cancer, multiple sclerosis, and strokes to such less serious illnesses as chronic back pain, headaches, and hay fever—immediately disappear in a few months. Though history is filled with these kinds of miraculous healings, what is different today is that everyone can experience them with a little instruction and support.

3. Learn as if you are a beginner. These miraculous healings are sustained by making a few significant dietary adjustments. To make these changes, we must open our minds and be willing to experiment and test out the dietary suggestions of the Natural Energy Diet (see chapter 13). By using this principle, we are motivated to learn something new, try it, and then discern for ourselves what works for us.

Without dietary changes a healing may not last. Symptoms go away in a healing session, but within a few days they may come back. If we continue to poison ourselves with just a few particular foods, the effect of a healing disappears almost as quickly as it was gained. With a few new insights about drinking and eating, and the practice of self-healing techniques, my clients and workshop participants have been automatically attracted to nutritious foods to rebuild and sustain a healthier body. After a healing takes place, healthy, nutritious food actually tastes better. For this reason, all the suggestions are easy to practice. They are sustained over time because they work immediately. When we try them, we will immediately begin to feel better.

Healing power does not make medicine obsolete in any way. Modern medicine, ancient healing practices, "alternative" medicine, and these new self-healing techniques, when used together in a complementary manner, can create even greater miraculous healings than any singular approach.

As you experience the immediate results of self-healing, you realize how little you really know about your potential to change and become excited about all the new possibilities that now exist. A whole new world opens up when we are willing to learn again as if we are beginners.

4. Love as if for the first time. In relationships, by using this guiding principle, many couples have found that miraculously they are once again falling in love with their partner.

They are able to forgive ex-partners and wish them well. The old resentments just melt away into the sunset of the past when we learn how to forgive. Everyone aspires to forgive but few have learned how to do it. The good intention to forgive is not enough; we must actually learn how to do it.

In the area of relationships, through teaching the ideas contained in *Men Are from Mars, Women Are from Venus*, I first began to notice the accelerated changes of this new age. Couples were finding that in a one-day workshop they were able to open their hearts to rekindle the love they thought was lost. Many marriages were saved. But even when relationships ended in divorce, couples were able to break up with greater love and forgiveness.

Creating lasting love doesn't mean that you will always stay married to the same person; it does mean you will always love that person and wish him or her well. People mistakenly blame themselves for failing in relationships when they get divorced, and yet some people find that after a divorce their lives have become more wonderful. Through forgiveness they were able to love freely again, as if they had never been hurt.

Thousands of couples at the brink of divorce have created lasting love by finding forgiveness and learning the skills for successful communication. When we feel that we are victims of love, this self-pity inevitably prevents us from opening our hearts and trusting love again. Fortunately, this old pain can be healed, and we can begin to love and trust again as if for the first time.

5. Give as if you already have what you need. With an understanding of their new potential for change, many have given up smoking or other unhealthy habits or addictions. Although they may have tried to stop in the past and failed, they are inspired to try again and this time succeed with an understanding of how to remove all addictive cravings. This time, by using this guiding principle, they are armed with a new arsenal of practical techniques, and it is easy to stop.

When you understand what creates miracles, you find that you already have the power to change and then follow through without difficulty and suffering. All that is required is an understanding of your new potential and a few new insights and techniques for awakening and using your inner power.

All addictions ultimately come from being overly dependent on someone or something outside of yourself to be happy. As you experience your inner power to get what you need, then you are not as dependent on others. You are then free to release addictive cravings.

As you give more while taking responsibility for your blocks, you begin to experience that it is through giving that you receive. For most of us, this concept is familiar but still just a concept. One cannot actually experience getting more through giving unless one is already self-sufficient.

If you are dependent on your partner to feel good, then when you give, some part of you needs and hopes to get something in return. Couples who primarily come together to fill up and not to give are always disappointed. The act of giving is eventually not as fulfilling because they are still dependent on receiving before they can feel good. Even when we are needy, giving can be very fulfilling in the beginning of a relationship, because we don't know our partner and we expect to get everything back. We naively expect perfection, which does not exist. Ultimately, instead of feeling energized by giving we become tired, empty, and exhausted. Whenever you feel resentment, it is a sign that you were giving to get something in return rather than giving from a sense of fullness without expectations or demands.

This explains the common perception that you can't really love another unless you first love yourself. Rather than depending on your partner to feel good, view him or her as a good dessert. You—not your partner—are responsible for supplying the important nutrients in your life. By loving yourself and having a fulfilling life first, the extra love your partner provides is an added bonus that you are not as dependent on. When you experience being independent and self-sufficient, you are able to give of yourself freely, not to expect a return, but to enjoy the fulfillment that comes from giving. You are able to give as if you already have what you need.

Women often think that they are giving without expecting something in return, but after a few years of feeling neglected in a relationship, they will complain in counseling, "I have given so much and have gotten nothing in return." The mistake is not in giving to her partner but rather in not taking the time to give to herself so that she is free to give to her partner without demanding more in return.

It is amazing how much more willing men are to give when they are asked for more in a nondemanding or nonresentful manner. It is practically impossible to ask for support in an easy, loving manner when we are not getting what we need. At those times, the secret to enjoying more of what our partner has to offer is first to give to ourselves whatever we need so that we are not dependent or demanding change from our partner.

6. Work as if money doesn't matter. The greatest miracle that I repeatedly observe is how quickly change can occur for people. It is not that every aspect of their life changes or gets better at once, but some significant aspect does. It may be that a woman is overweight, experiencing low energy, feeling deprived in her relationship, and not liking her job. It doesn't all get better at once.

Some will begin to lose weight right away, but others begin to love themselves and their partner more, and then, at a later time, they begin to lose weight or change jobs. Sometimes, before we can make a life change, we first need to make an attitude change. Sometimes when a physical healing does not occur, it is not until we experience an attitude shift about work that the body heals. Using this sixth guiding principle, many people begin to experience their power to create practical miracles.

Although we live in an age of miracles, it is still true that change occurs gradually. It still takes time for the seed to grow into a tree. Everything doesn't change at once. The miracle is that now the blocks to natural change and healing can be easily removed. The seeds of greatness in our hearts now can grow freely at their natural rate into a beautiful tree.

Sometimes before a physical sickness clears up, an emotional issue must be healed. At other times, a physical sickness is miraculously healed, and then the buried emotional issues responsible for that sickness begin to surface. In a similar manner, sometimes a person can make a life change or change of habit first, and then the emotional issues begin to surface in order to be healed. Or, it may be that first the emotional issue becomes healed and released, and then the necessary life change becomes clear, and we are naturally motivated to make the change.

In most cases, when it comes to healing the body, some emotional change must first occur. This explains why some people get a more dramatic physical healing than others do. They come to the healing more emotionally vulnerable and open to being helped or healed. In a similar way, when it comes to being more successful in life, some attitudinal changes need to occur first. By first learning to change our attitude, our power to create outer change in our life dramatically changes.

If every day we go to work because we need the money and not because it makes us feel good, then we are disconnecting from our inner power. By not following our heart and freely choosing our work, we create our own misery and sickness. On the other hand, when we are free to work, not primarily for the money but because it makes us feel good, then our greatest power to change our circumstances comes forward.

This explains why some wealthy people just get richer. They

work not because they need the money but to serve others in a way that makes them feel good. When wealthy people get sick or lose their wealth, it is often because they stop working. Since they don't have to work, they lose their motivation to work. As a direct result, they often become soft, lazy, unproductive, unhappy, sick, or experience substance abuse.

More commonly, people spend their lives working for the money so that one day they can retire and stop working. When we work for the money, then, if we make a lot of money or we retire, our tendency is to stop working. This is a particularly common scenario for men. We stop working because we don't have to work anymore, and very quickly we get sick and die. Insurance companies have observed that men tend to die three years after retirement. Having a lot of money and the time to do what we want to do is great if we also have the motivation to continue working in service of others in some meaningful manner.

Rather than seeking to change circumstances to feel good, the secret of creating miracles is first to change your attitude without depending on outer circumstances to change. If we are dependent on a job to pay our bills, then the first step is to begin awakening our power to be more fulfilled with our circumstances the way they are. Once we can appreciate the opportunities we do have, then miraculously new opportunities begin to present themselves that allow us to express more of who we are and to create the opportunity for greater success.

When you work as if money doesn't matter as much, your decisions come from your own set of values and not from those of others. You are free to be yourself and do what your conscience and sense of duty dictates. With this awareness, we can work as if money doesn't matter even though we do need the money to pay our bills. With this attitude shift, we still need money from our work, but the primary reason we work is to express ourselves in service to the world in some meaningful way.

7. **Relax as if everything will be okay.** Workshop participants often report that life is freer from struggle. Extreme mood swings transform so that we are easily able to manage our ups and downs. As you learn to purify your body and release old toxins, unhealthy cravings are replaced with healthy desires. As you begin to experience your miraculous inner potential, then fear, worry, panic, and anxiety lessen and eventually disappear.

With this amazing transformation, circumstances that would have caused fear or anxiety now generate a sense of relaxed calm and enthusiasm. One feels again (or for the first time) the innocence of a confident young adult ready to leave home and take on the challenges and enjoy the wonders of a new and exciting life.

Grounded in our true selves, we are able to relax in our lives even in the midst of turmoil, helplessness, and uncertainty as if we know with certainty that everything will turn out okay. The ultimate truth is that everything eventually does turn out to be okay. Yes, we experience loss, and, yes, we make mistakes, but by healing our wounds and facing our challenges with an open heart, we discover that every experience offers a growth opportunity to us. Gradually, one learns to remain alert, as if one were in danger, but relaxed, as if everything will be okay. When we approach crises with inner calm, we are much more effective at finding solutions than we would be if we were experiencing anxiety and fear.

8. **Talk to God as if you are being heard.** Literally within a few hours most participants in my Practical Miracles workshop have a tangible experience that God, or whatever they choose to refer to as their spiritual or guiding source, immediately responds to their requests. Even those who are uncomfortable with using or hearing the word "God" experience the incredible natural energy that is always surrounding us. It is this energy that heals a wound or inspires greatness. Though I

personally call this intelligent and responsive energy "God," participants are free to call it by any name.

Suddenly the notion of right or wrong concepts and confusion about God disappear or become irrelevant when you have the direct experience. When the pain you have felt for nine years disappears, you suddenly become a believer, not by someone telling you what is right, but because you have directly experienced it.

With the simple technique of recharging, participants immediately experience this natural healing energy by following a simple procedure for asking for help. Within minutes, a pleasing energy begins to flow into their bodies through their fingertips. Once aware of this energy, they can direct it to release all stress, distress, resistance, and pain in their mind, heart, soul, and body.

By learning to feel this energy, you automatically connect with your true inner potential. The doorway to increasing success is opened. Good fortune and greater competence always comes to those who listen to the whispers of their hearts and follow through with their impulses to change. Many people in my seminars have noticed that when they are more confident and motivated, they experience greater success and good luck in making their dreams come true.

The reason good and loving actions can create good fortune is that they require us to open our hearts, and then the miraculous power can be better accessed. It is often easier for those who have tried to do good to feel more of this energy. Sometimes, however, it is more difficult. They have tried so hard in life always to be loving that they have disconnected from their occasional negative feelings. By suppressing negativity, they have lessened their ability to feel altogether.

Without a feeling heart, one cannot experience the energy and begin immediately to benefit from it. Fortunately, there are simple techniques to awaken one's ability to feel fully. Regardless of one's mistakes or history, everyone quickly gets access. It is everyone's birthright and is immediately available when you know where to look.

Good fortune is the nature of life. It is only when we persist in going against our heart that we miss out on all that life is ready to give us. With the ability to open your heart and mind, you gain the power to release struggle in your life and to turn the inevitable dramas and crises into opportunities to learn lessons and to grow stronger.

As you begin to follow your personal dreams, you begin to experience an enormous amount of creativity. With this incredible flow, you realize that you really "don't do it," but that it *happens through you.* At this point, the experience of God and God's miraculous creative power becomes a direct experience, feeling, or perception rather than just a concept. At this point, when you pray, you will know with complete certainty that you are talking to God as if you are being heard, and you will get help immediately.

As you experience this flow, the struggle leaves your life. Whenever people struggle, ultimately it is because they have forgotten or disconnected with the great power or God that works through all of us and in nature. It is as though you have purchased a new car and, instead of starting it up and driving away, you get out and start pushing it on your own.

In my workshops, generally speaking, 90 percent of the audience can easily experience natural healing energy and immediately begin drawing it in. For most people, it is a completely new experience. Some others simply need a little more practice, while yet others need to find their own different approach.

Remember: One way is not for everyone. I do not consider it a failure when someone doesn't have the experience others have. I know people are different and that my way is not the best for everyone. I always say a prayer for them and wish them well, trusting that with this greater awareness of what they want, they will be able to attract it into their life in some other form.

When people use these simple techniques, suddenly God or a higher power is no longer a concept to be thought about or discussed, but a direct experiential reality. Once you can feel God's natural energy flowing in through your fingertips, then you can begin using God's support to heal yourself and those you care about. As you continue to use this energy to change yourself, you can use it to increase creativity, success, and good fortune. This is what was meant in the past by getting the blessings of a saint or a "boon" from the gods. When you can feel this energy, you can direct it and immediately see the benefits.

9. Feast as if you can have whatever you want. By applying easy dietary changes and the self-healing technique of decharging, many overweight participants have shed unwanted pounds in a few months. Using new techniques, extra weight drops off, as you eat as much as you want. Even when you are overweight, as 70 percent of Americans are, by eating more, you can restore your body to its ideal healthy weight.

Miraculous change doesn't require any sacrifice. To lose weight, boring or tedious exercise regimes are not necessary. I personally lost thirty pounds in two months without any exercise program. Once I regained my healthy weight, I started wanting to exercise my body and use it more. It is no wonder that overweight people have a difficult time sticking to exercise programs. Pushing an unhealthy overweight body to exercise sometimes is an additional strain and is not only unhealthy but also unnecessary. Once you lose your extra weight, you will want to create opportunities to exercise, because it feels good and keeps your body strong and vibrant.

Once you can experience your natural desire, with a little guidance you discover that you can eat as much as you want of the foods that you want without any sacrifice. This wonderful abundant state is created after giving up your addictions to just a few very unhealthy foods.

Putting It All Together

By using each of the nine guiding principles as they fit and work for you, and by regular practice of the natural energy self-healing techniques, you can and will begin to see practical benefits right away. Some people already may be using some of the guiding principles, but, until they find and apply the missing ingredient, they are still blocked from accessing their inner power to create miracles. Some already may be using all of the principles but are not aware of the simple advanced techniques of practical miracles. With one small change, they become unblocked and suddenly experience the benefits they have been working so hard to achieve.

If you read through the list and panic because you are not already using them, don't despair. All it takes is to make one change in the right direction and you will see remarkable results. It is amazing how quickly the results come when you make the right change for you, which also happens to be an easy change. Change is difficult when you are not accessing your miraculous power. Difficult practices actually block your miraculous power. In the past, difficulty was needed, but now everything has changed, and it is only the easy approaches that work. If something seems too difficult, then look in a different direction. If this approach is right for you, you will experience that the different techniques of practical miracles are not complex or difficult, and they begin working right away.

4

SPIRITUAL ALGEBRA

In the past, miraculous results could not be sustained, simply because most people were not ready. Everything real in life unfolds gradually, in stages. A seed cannot turn into a tree until it is ready. It takes nurturing and time. In our past stages of growth, mankind could only glimpse what was possible. Now we are fully ready to comprehend the truth and express our inner potential to create miracles. The stage of glimpsing is now complete. We are blessed to be alive at a time when miracles are possible for everyone.

One way to understand this global shift is using the concept of world consciousness. Einstein first popularized this notion. He said the new and advanced ideas that took him years to comprehend would, in later generations, be comprehended by children. This change in our global capability to understand, he explained, begins when one person makes a shift toward greater awareness in a new direction.

Like a snowball rolling down a hill, an idea whose time has

come eventually gathers more and more snow, growing in size exponentially. Likewise, as more people expand their comprehension, at a certain point, the entire world consciousness changes. As a result, what was considered radical or at the level of genius in one age becomes common sense when the whole world catches on.

This helps describe the shift that we have just experienced. When you heat water, at a certain point it begins to boil and turn into steam. In a practical sense, society has been simmering for the last two hundred years. Now the water has begun to boil and the radical change from water to steam is happening. A change has occurred in the world's consciousness that allows us to comprehend and feel more. With this shift, the whole world is now capable of creating practical miracles.

It is important to understand how and why this shift in our abilities came about. Without that insight, we may not be sufficiently motivated to make changes when we have failed so many times before. Even though all will eventually make this shift, why be the last? It is now your choice.

This shift into an age of practical miracles is analogous to a radical change that occurs in almost every child when he or she becomes a teenager. By observing this more familiar and common transformation, we can best interpret our new reality.

One of the many dramatic shifts and growth spurts around age thirteen is the sudden ability to understand algebra. After many years of cerebral development, in one day a switch in the brain is turned on that allows the new teenager to go from concrete thinking to the capacity to comprehend abstract thought.

Although the brain has spent years developing to prepare for this shift, the actual change occurs in a moment. There is no gradual unfolding. It is a leap. Prior to this magic instant, all attempts to comprehend algebra tend to be a disappointing struggle unless the child is particularly gifted in math. For all children, after this sudden shift, learning algebra becomes easy if the support and instruction are available.

**Learning algebra is most difficult when it is taught
before the student is ready.**

It is important to keep in mind that this shift literally
occurs in one day. If this new ability is not used, then the
part of the brain responsible for abstract thinking doesn't
have a chance to develop. This shift is analogous to a change
that has just happened in the world.

If the student's brain has not yet made the necessary shift
from concrete thinking to abstract thinking, then he just can't
learn algebra, even if the teacher is great. Trying to learn before
the brain is ready can make matters even worse. Instead of
understanding that he is just not ready to learn, a student may
mistakenly conclude that he is inadequate and *cannot* learn.
This mistaken belief can block his power. Positive belief and
expectancy is necessary for any ability to develop.

**Trying to learn something before the brain is ready
can make matters even worse.**

This shift in brainpower is analogous to the change that
has just occurred in our world consciousness. Developing
your capacity to create practical miracles is like learning
algebra, but it is actually a kind of spiritual algebra. One
day we can't learn it, and the next day we can.

In comparing your new power to create practical miracles with learning algebra, remember, it is just an analogy. If
you were not good at math, it doesn't mean you are not
ready to create miracles. And if algebra was difficult for
you, it probably was either taught before you were ready, or
you just didn't get the right instruction and support. Children have different learning styles. When you were growing

up, most teachers didn't have the knowledge or the time to nurture children's many needs in order for them to learn more effectively.

Recognizing Your Potential

Radical change in potential cannot be directly perceived or recognized. When teenagers shift in their capacity to understand algebra, there is no outward or inward indication. It is not like the radical growth spurts that occur in the night, which are physically noticeable the next day.

When the switch of abstract thinking is turned on, teenagers don't wake up feeling in any way different. They neither look different nor do they sense a change in attitude. They do not know they now have the ability to comprehend and learn algebra. The only way to detect their new capacity and recognize their potential is to begin using it.

In a very similar manner, our new capacity to create miracles does not change us in any way. We do not feel at all different. Yet, once we are given the opportunity to identify this capacity and use it, it can be felt and increased. This is what education and training is about. To awaken our miraculous powers, we merely need to know that they exist and to start looking for them. Without this awareness, we will never begin the journey.

To awaken our miraculous powers, we just need to know that they exist and to start looking for them.

Our capacity to do miracles has been quietly developing for thousands of years but has suddenly arrived. It started flickering on and off about two hundred years ago when people first experienced the urge for freedom and democracy.

As our miraculous powers began to stir, we came to believe

that all men and women were equal and that each person had the capacity to create his or her own destiny. People were no longer like children who needed to be ruled by others but had the capacity to rule their own lives. Although this was our vision, we were not yet fully able to achieve it because, like a new teenager, we were still waffling. We would get glimpses of what was possible and then be unable to follow through and hold on to the new possibilities and values.

Throughout the world, real and lasting changes are occurring to open the door for everyone to develop this new and latent power to create our own future. We no longer are limited by genes, size, color, sex, race, family status, or religious background. Democracy, or at least a movement in that direction, exists everywhere. There are global signs of this transformation. Even people in oppressed countries are at last standing up for their rights and seeking the equality available with increasing freedom. Miraculous change is now possible for all.

Interest in God and Religion

Unless someone teaches teenagers the basics of algebra, they will not know they have this new ability. They may spend the rest of their lives thinking they can't do algebra, thus never taking the time to learn. All they will be sure of is that the old math based on concrete thinking seems boring. As a result, they may become disinterested in math altogether.

In a similar manner, many people today have become bored and disinterested in religion, spirituality, and God, simply because they were not presented a message that reflected their new abilities and understandings. People who ridicule spiritual pursuit or the notion of God, or who have given up on personal change, are often in some ways more advanced souls. They are analogous to kids who go through puberty a little earlier than most. Although they don't have long to wait until the others make the shift, they will still be very different from their peers and more advanced. While they are more advanced in some ways because they don't have a lot of peer support, they often will have more problems.

People who ridicule spiritual pursuit are sometimes more advanced souls.

During the last few hundred years, a small percentage of the population of the world started making this shift. These "advanced souls" were the great leaders, innovators, inventors, artists, writers, revolutionaries, scientists, and spiritual teachers. Although they shined brighter, they were really not much more advanced. In the bigger picture of evolution, when compared to millions of years of evolution, a hundred years is but a blink of the eye. Within a few hundred years the rest of mankind would catch up and all would be at the same level once again.

In the last fifty years this shift has occurred for a much greater percentage of the world's population. Millions have gone through the change. And now, in this new millennium, billions have just made the shift and are ready to use their advanced potential.

Changing ahead of the rest of mankind is not always a comfortable experience. The more advanced souls often were left out, mistrusted, isolated, or even burned at the stake for being different. Ask any girl who is the first in her group to have her period. Because she is in the minority, this new and wondrous change often is associated with shame, confusion, embarrassment, and the fear of rejection.

In the past, when a soul was ready to create practical miracles and there were no teachers to lead the way, it could be very disheartening. Such people knew something was missing but didn't know what it was or where to find it. The traditional religions were still preaching an appropriate message for the masses, but not for them.

Using our algebra analogy, spiritual teachers and religious leaders still were teaching concrete math skills, and some souls were now beyond them. It was difficult to find an advanced teacher that could challenge their new capacity to comprehend life and its mysteries. They needed spiritual algebra. These advanced souls were seeking a higher truth and often turned away from traditional spirituality because what they were being told about God was not right for them. While some went searching for truth in unorthodox or unconventional ways, others just lost interest.

**In the past, those who professed
to have the spiritual answers were
still teaching the message for the masses.**

For a slightly older soul to accept many of the old beliefs being taught about God, it was similar to a teenager being expected to believe that a chubby Santa Claus, dressed in red and transported by flying reindeer, really comes down the chimney in every home around the world in one night and distributes presents to every good child. For the older soul it was time to move on to a more advanced understanding.

Most religions and theologies have been advancing and changing but too slowly for the more advanced souls. The old ways of thinking were too restrictive and no longer relevant. The slightly older souls needed something to challenge their new potential to create miracles and thereby stimulate and empower themselves. They wanted to feel the power to make their dreams come true. If their religion didn't show them how, they looked elsewhere.

If their religion didn't make people feel good about themselves, then they looked elsewhere.

During the last two hundred years, and particularly in the last fifty years, an increasing number of people changed to a different religion, joined a newly formed religion, started their own religion, or simply pulled away from organized religion to join the new "religions" of science and technology, consumerism, pop culture, psychology and therapy, environmentalism, holistic medicine, or the budding self-help movement, complete with books, manuals, experts, healers, diets, support groups, twelve-step programs, and workshops.

Many traditional places of worship stopped being functional and often became tourist spots or simply gathering places. The churches and temples that still thrive are generally led by advanced souls who are open to the new insights entering the human consciousness. They honor and include new values that come from science, psychology, and the self-help movement.

Those people who were disillusioned or just disinterested in spirituality, dismissed the notion of a Divine Being, as it was being taught, and looked elsewhere for something that could stimulate and challenge the new potential they were suddenly sensing. In many cases, they unnecessarily threw out the notion of God and spirituality. They threw out the baby with the bath water.

Rejecting the notion of God is like throwing out the baby with the bath water.

Even without "conscious" help from God or the divine

power of the universe, advanced souls were sometimes able to use their new potential to manifest outer creative and technological miracles. It is common for many great scientists to be agnostic or atheistic. They often achieved incredible greatness and creativity in their careers but failed in their personal lives. They experienced intense distress or physical sickness. Others focused on some secret, esoteric practice for the advanced and found great inner peace, but they were unable to find success in the outer world and lived in poverty or sickness.

The West is filled with outwardly successful people. They may have it all in the outer world, but for many it is never enough to make them happy. They take medications to suppress their pain and are still bitter from vicious divorce settlements. Their children don't talk to them, and they wonder: Is this all there is? In a practical sense they have the potential for learning spiritual algebra but have not found a good "algebra teacher" to awaken their potential to create success in *all* areas of life.

Technology Mirrors Our New Potential

The inner change, which has now occurred in all people, is in many ways reflected in the outer changes we can witness today. For example, as the inner consciousness of all mankind has expanded to a new level, the whole world is suddenly connected by TV, cellular phones, and, most recently, by the Internet. Now almost everyone in the world will have access to these newly developed technological marvels and miracles. As people acknowledge they have the consciousness to know the truth within themselves, suddenly a mountain of information is available to anyone with a computer and an Internet connection.

What technological miracles we now have are very impressive, but they are only just the beginning. There are so many new innovations, improvements, advances, and discoveries that are already in the pipeline. In a similar manner, everyone now has access to his inner ability to create miracles. It is only a very short time before we will be able to use that ability and make incredible advances in our own lives. What we can do today in our inner and outer worlds will dramatically increase with every year. I have already witnessed it in my own personal life and in the lives of workshop participants. I see it not just in my work, but also in the work of other healers and teachers.

Those of us who started using personal computers twenty years ago have had to suffer with slow processing speeds and limited storage space. To secure even the smallest advancement, we always had to pay dearly. Today, we buy computers at a fraction of the cost we used to pay, and these machines are not only smaller, lighter, easier to use, and light-years faster, but they are also capable of storing all the data we could ever imagine. Most important, they are not prone to crashing all the time as the older ones did.

Even though you may be an expert at using the old models, if you don't upgrade you will be behind the times. And the newest computers are equally available to all. In a similar way, a much higher ability to experience and develop our inner miraculous powers is now available to everyone.

It doesn't matter how spiritually advanced you are or how loving and good you have been. Even if you have "never sinned" or at least tried really hard not to, it doesn't give you an advantage. It doesn't make you somehow more worthy for developing this potential. Everyone has equal access. You may have wasted your life squandering your potential, repeatedly making the same mistakes, and over-looking your inner gifts, but it is never too late to benefit from this new universal blessing. No one is denied entrance and there is no price to pay. This new inner technology is already yours.

> **The power to change our lives is available to all of us.**

Even spending years on a technique of inner development to access this new power doesn't give you an extra advantage. You don't get a special pass that lets you go to the front of the line. There is no line at all. Certainly, you have been enjoying the benefit of your path, but, unless you have been making lots of changes and innovations in your practice, it is probably now time to upgrade. That doesn't mean you have to turn in the old computer; instead, you can just insert a new hard drive or the latest faster chip. In a similar manner, we don't have to scrap our past; we just need to update and upgrade to access the new potential available to all of us.

> **We don't have to scrap our past; we just need to update and upgrade.**

The beautiful religious traditions have so much to offer if we can simply reinterpret some of their restrictive and limiting aspects and forgive their abuses and corruption. Rejecting religion is like rejecting Beethoven, just because we like country-western music or because Beethoven didn't play an electric guitar. Why not respect and enjoy it all?

> **Rejecting religion is like rejecting Beethoven just because we like country-western music or rock and roll.**

It is not necessary to reinvent the wheel. We don't need a new religion. We don't need another parent to teach us what is right or what the rules are. We just need to open our hearts and minds. We all have within ourselves the potential to determine what is right or wrong for ourselves. Two thousand years ago, Jesus shocked the establishment when he said the law of God is already written in your heart. In a similar manner, when we learn to use our new potential and to open our hearts, we are then not dependent on anyone but ourselves to reveal to us what is true.

By looking within ourselves, we can know the truth and develop our inner power to create practical miracles. Following your heart and not outside teachings, traditions, or feedback doesn't mean you don't listen or respect. It means you listen and then follow what you feel is right for you. By continuing to follow your heart and doing what you love, through trial and error, you will gradually learn what is right for you. It is not possible to know what is right or wrong until you have experienced what you are talking about.

Without direct experience, you certainly can have an opinion, but you cannot *know*. From this perspective, you can really never know what is right for another. You may have an accurate opinion, but you cannot really *know*. All we can really ever know for sure is what is good for us, and that too will change as we change.

As you find the truth within, you will suddenly start seeing it in all religions. You will understand the underlying message is always the same. You will be aware of how that truth was misinterpreted by others who came later or by translators who didn't fully comprehend the message. You also will recognize that some messages are just no longer appropriate.

The ultimate truth about life is like a river. It is always the same water, but it also is always shifting and changing. A river never flows in a straight line for long, but, instead, it naturally weaves back and forth. It also takes on the mood of the day. If the sun is shining, then the water is a beautiful blue, while on a cloudy day it appears dark and gray. Although it appears different, it is not. Water is always water. It may be hot or cold, clear or murky, but it is still water. In a similar way, the same truth can be found in every religion. Once you have tasted the water, regardless of how different it appears to be, you know it is the same refreshing and life-giving water of life.

**As you find the truth within,
suddenly you start seeing it in all religions.**

To found a new religion is to deny the value of other religions. At this point in history, it is not necessary. Anyone who feels the need to start a new faith is clearly not qualified. If a person were capable of knowing the truth, then he or she would already see the value of our present religions and not feel compelled to form another. Rather than a new, better religion, we are ready to experience the underlying truth that is present in every religion, and through that experience provide a unifying basis to support peace and harmony in the world.

We must clearly recognize that anyone who professes to have the one way or best way is not fit to lead the way. Certainly, they may have the best way for them or their following, but not for all. It is an outdated notion to believe there is one way for all. It is this limited belief that actually prevents us from experiencing our inner power to create practical miracles in our personal life and in the world. To move forward, we must open our minds and hearts to allow and respect differences in all areas of life.

When established religions were closed to change, new religions were needed to create an adjustment suitable to time and place. Now every religion is filled with leaders who have this new ability and will soon recognize it. As religions open up, they, too, will see the truth in all other traditions with respect and appreciation. While maintaining their own unique rituals and traditions, they will be able to honor other traditions as well. The notions of superiority, chosen people, or "our way is the best way" will simply disappear. This is already happening in some places, but now it will happen globally.

From Analog to Digital

In this new age of practical miracles change is greatly accelerated. Changes that may have taken years to achieve now can be made easily and instantly. In this sense, we have shifted from being analog to digital. There is no need to rewind tapes slowly. With the touch of a button, we are back to the beginning. We can move wherever we want to go. If there is something on a CD or DVD that you want to skip, then presto—in an instant you are where you want to be.

Think about one of the oldest truisms: Time heals all wounds. Just wait long enough and things will get better. Well, now you don't have to wait. Push the right button on the right equipment and you will instantly be there. The secret is in updating your equipment and learning how to use it.

By their thirties, many people have given up thinking they can change. They no longer make resolutions, because they have failed to follow through so many times before. Why bother promising to change if it is only for a few weeks? Rather than suffer the humiliation of repeated failure, we lose our innocent exuberance to be better and happier.

Caring and Trust

In a like manner, when other people have let us down, we give up believing that change is possible. We give up trying to get the support we need. This commonly happens more clearly in intimate relationships. First we feel disappointed, then we lose hope for change. As a result, men often stop caring, while women stop trusting. Both attitudes block us from feeling the love that brought us together in the first place. In all areas of life, when we stop caring or trusting, we disconnect with our inner power to create change.

When we give up the hope for change, men often stop caring, while women stop trusting.

Instead of making the needed changes and adjustments in our relationships, work, and personal habits, we resign ourselves to mediocrity by passively accepting our conditions. At a certain point, we surrender to the limiting belief that we cannot change or that lasting change is not possible. This is what often makes us get sick when we grow older.

Often men stop caring when they fail to please their partner over time. When she is happy, he is happy, but when she is displeased, he begins to feel like a failure and shuts down. He feels, "Why bother? Nothing I do is ever enough."

In this example, he cares too much and is too dependent on his partner's responses. To remedy the situation, he needs to adjust his unrealistic expectations and unloving demands while also taking more time on his own to feel good about himself without being so dependent on her. With this simple change, he can be disappointed occasionally without having to stop caring altogether.

Women, on the other hand, trust too much, and then when they become disappointed, they stop trusting. Like men with caring, women either fully trust or close up and stop trusting altogether. When she gets what she needs in a relationship, then she begins to depend on that fulfillment and mistakenly stops finding fulfillment in other areas of her life. This kind of dependence is unhealthy. As a result, when he disappoints her, rather than trusting that he did his best, she closes up and doesn't trust at all.

**Expecting one person to fulfill all our needs
is unrealistic and leads to unloving demands.**

At such times, rather than trusting a man to fulfill her, a woman needs to begin trusting herself and God. This trust grows as she begins to experience her new potential for greatness within herself. This inner confidence frees her from too much dependence on her partner for her fulfillment. Eventually she learns to trust a partner appropriately, without unrealistic expectations or unloving demands.

If we (both men and women) are not dependent on our partners for our happiness, then when they frustrate or disappoint us in some way, it is like a little ripple of upset on an ocean of love, respect, appreciation, understanding, acceptance, caring, and trust. It is normal to feel bothered, annoyed, or even irritated sometimes by the people we love. The secret of marital happiness is learning just to let it go and freely love once again. Whenever we feel loving, we are back to our true self.

To connect with this free expression of love, think about how you felt in the beginning of the relationship or in a really good friendship. If your partner or friend disappointed you, your immediate response was, "It's okay." This wonderful loving reaction occurs only when we are not too dependent or when we are confident that we can get what we need in our life. By directly experiencing your power to create miracles, you can gradually wean yourself from being too dependent on others.

To heal overdependence, besides looking inside ourselves for fulfillment, we must also occasionally look outside the relationship for fun and friendship. It is not healthy when your mate is your only best friend or when you always do everything together. It is important to sustain a separate life as well. Just as parents need to carve out special time together without their children, so do couples need to carve out special time for themselves to do what they love without their partner.

Besides looking inside ourselves for fulfillment, we must also occasionally look outside the relationship for fun and friendship.

When we are not so dependent on our partner for everything, we are then capable of adjusting our unrealistic expectations and unloving demands. We become forgiving of our partner's mistakes and more accepting of his or her limitations and differences. When this occurs, a woman can easily and appropriately trust a man to do his best, while a man can continue to care about and consider his partner's needs, but not so much that he loses himself.

As we move into this new twenty-first century, both men and women will be less dependent on each other and thereby more loving and accepting of their differences. It is this new, more liberated expression of love that will allow romance and passion to thrive for a lifetime.

Creating a Lifetime of Love

Already people are feeling the possibility of lasting romance and passion. Never in history have couples expected passion to last in a marriage, but today people do. Though this is a possibility, we still have a lot to learn about how to achieve this miracle of love. To achieve a new kind of relationship, we have to open our minds and hearts to accepting and embracing our differences. We have to reeducate ourselves from the conditioning of our past generations. If we want to yield a new crop, we have to plant a new seed. By thinking and doing things differently from previous generations, we can create a different result.

Without a way of creating lasting passion, rather than continuing to stay married because people were "supposed to," couples separated, and the divorce rate suddenly jumped from 10 to 50 percent thirty years ago. Though Americans continue to get married, in some countries the rate of marriage has dropped significantly.

The increase of divorce and disillusionment regarding marriage in the Western world did not occur because people were less loving, but because they had higher standards. They knew more was possible but didn't know how to achieve it . . . yet. Just as some left a marriage in search of something more, others left their traditional spiritual support system.

Now, as couples learn to release their unrealistic expectations and unloving demands instead of leaving their partners, many couples will be able to update their old ways and make changes with even greater ease. By being less dependent and giving themselves and their partners more freedom to have their own life as well, the dream of lasting love will become a practical reality. With a little practice and some new insights, millions of couples have already benefited from the simple, commonsense approach in *Men Are from Mars, Women Are from Venus* and other popular relationship guides. The understanding and acceptance of gender differences has given new hope to millions of couples.

Religious Openness

Just as our minds and hearts are opening up in our relationships, religious institutions are opening up as well. Another example of new religious openness is that these institutions are not closed to many new insights and adjustments suggested by popular self-help writers. Even the most fundamental and conservative religious groups often recommend my books on relationships and dating as well as those of other popular self-help teachers or self-styled spiritual teachers.

Religious leaders know people are having problems, and they recognize the importance of new information. People commonly tell me it was their minister, preacher, pastor, rabbi, swami, or guru who recommended my books on love, dating, healing, success, and parenting. This is not an admission of failure on religion's part, but an expression of the new global consciousness. The world has changed; mankind has changed. It is time to update and learn from each other and ourselves rather than from one source outside ourselves.

Religious leaders know people are having problems and recognize the importance of new information.

In my direct experience, more and more religious leaders are making the needed adjustments in this new age. Just as people now are capable of changing, so are religions. If you have left your childhood faith, you would be amazed to see how much it has evolved. This new capacity for change is not just for the young, it is for the old as well.

As religions are being challenged to change, so are the people who have left their childhood faith. It is time to let go of our limiting judgments and fears, and appreciate our differences while recognizing the one underlying universal truth. If you have left your religion, expand your horizons by taking the time to see if the new truths you have realized are present there as well.

If you follow a liberal spiritual approach, it is fine to disagree but it is hypocritical to judge fundamentalist or conservative religions as being too judgmental. While some need a more liberal approach, others legitimately need a more conservative path. To grow in your miraculous power, your mind must be open to see the truth in every religion. Certainly there will be things that you find limiting, but rather than focus on the differences, find the underlying truth. As you rely on yourself to discern what you find to be true, you are directly strengthening and exercising your connection with the divine within you.

Remember that gold is gold, no matter what form it is shaped into. The ultimate truths about life can be expressed in many different ways, but they are still the ultimate truths. Each religion shapes the truth for people of different temperaments and stages of growth. There is no better religion. Take the time to experience the truth in all religions. By respecting the differences in others and finding the underlying unity, you will be setting yourself free to be different while also staying in harmony with the world. This is the promise of the new millennium.

While there are infinite ways to climb a mountain, there is only one top. It's time to realize that we are there. Now we need to unpack and enjoy the view of new and endless possibilities. It is time to buckle up and hold on for a very exciting ride.

Everyone now has the power to create practical miracles in their own lives. However, like algebra, it requires learning from a good teacher. By understanding the nine guiding principles for creating practical miracles, you will immediately experience amazing growth and change. Let *How to Live for Change and Change for Life* be your algebra workbook to remind you of your new powers and assist you in developing your new potential. Since the time is right, all it takes is a few explanations and some simple techniques and exercises, and you will be well on your way.

5

LIVING IN
AN AGE OF MIRACLES

The nine principles of creating miracles have been lived in various ways with varying degrees of clarity throughout the ages. What is different today is our new capacity to comprehend them all at the same time and to directly experience their practical value. These principles are no longer concepts we hope to achieve some day after a long search or much practice. They can now be directly experienced and quickly become our common experience. A dramatic shift of enormous historic proportions has occurred. We are now living in an age of miracles.

Dramatic changes in society are not new. Throughout history, society has always made radical changes and developments. Each new age has delivered some new development, from the pure but rigid righteousness of the Victorian Age to the bloody revolutions of people fighting for freedom.

Each period of change has brought some new ideal to be

expressed in religion as well as in the arts and sciences. Whether we were envisioning new and better ways to govern or were creating the new inventions responsible for the Industrial Age or now the Digital Age, mankind was always growing in its ability to create practical miracles.

What is different about the last two hundred years, and particularly the last fifty years, is the accelerated speed of change. Our capacity to comprehend more has allowed change to occur more rapidly. In ages past, significant trends and the development of major realizations took hundreds of years. In the last two hundred years, with the birth of democracy, change began to occur more quickly. As we approached the new millennium, the pace of change increased even more. This rapid change opened the door for a new and different level of consciousness for all mankind.

The Nature of Progress

For every advance throughout history, mankind always faced new problems. Although the next advance solved the old problems, new problems were created. This is the nature of progress, and it also demonstrates why one good idea is never enough on its own. Too much of a good thing is not good.

**Taking anything to an extreme
defeats its original purpose.**

When one principle is taken to an extreme, we tend to discard it altogether, because of the problems it creates, and adopt a new principle, which happens to be the solution. If society becomes too rigid, then it shifts to being more open and free. When it becomes too conservative or traditional, then it shifts to being more liberal and innovative. History is filled with these shifts. Today something new is happening.

We are now capable of comprehending difference not as a threat, but as potential support.

Just as a pendulum swings back and forth and finally finds its resting place, mankind has arrived at its resting point of balance.

We are at the balance point between opposite movements. We are at that magic moment between night and day. We have awakened to a new age of practical miracles. What was impossible to comprehend before will now be easy. Old principles need not be thrown out because they conflict with new ideas. Instead, the old and new can be integrated into a whole that is much greater than the sum of its parts.

Men Are from Mars, Women Are from Venus

The widespread acceptance of the ideas of *Men Are from Mars, Women Are from Venus* is a good example of this change. When I first introduced these ideas in the early eighties, I met with enormous resistance. Many people just were not ready to accept my ideas. If I talked about the difference between men and women, it frequently was interpreted to mean that I was saying one sex was better than the other. Some people felt I wanted to bring back traditional ideas and suppress the new concepts of freedom and equal opportunity.

Now, almost everyone who has experienced being in an intimate relationship is very accepting of the notion that men and women are different and that these differences are good, though sometimes difficult to deal with. Our age-old views about gender differences have indeed radically changed. Not only do we accept the notion that men and women are different, but at the same time we have embraced a completely new assumption that these differences don't mean that one is better than the other.

A higher principle has been realized from this integration of opposing ideas. Men and women can be different and equal. Once we realize this, we can clearly see that, unless we recognize these differences, we cannot equally honor the human rights of each person. This is the same consciousness that can and will say black and white can be different and equal. All religions—East and West, old and new—can be different and equal. It is this one shift that literally can change the world forever and provide a real basis for lasting peace and justice.

Overcoming Resistance

What allowed people to accept in a nonthreatening manner the simple message of *Men Are from Mars* was the way in which it was presented. Every point was based on common experiences and had practical value. Those people who shared these common experiences could immediately grasp these ideas.

When we can experience the truth for ourselves, we are not so dependent on others to guide or teach us. With access to the truth within, we can release the need to find the one and best way and easily move into what works for ourselves. We are not threatened by differences, but instead welcome and attempt to appreciate them.

With access to the truth within, we are not threatened by differences, but instead welcome them.

When some intellectuals attempted to debate me, I saw it as a waste of my time. I would simply point out that my message was not for everyone, but that in my experience, what I suggested was helpful to many men and women. When they demanded proof, as everyone should, I simply said my ideas were based on plain old common sense. These doubters were so used to the old way of depending on the stamp of academic approval that they couldn't conceive of something new and good coming from common sense. My findings were criticized for not being the result of a double-blind study with references to ten other experts who had done similar research.

Although research is very helpful in expanding our awareness and pointing us in different directions, the results don't inevitably mean something is true. Believing only in research is like waiting for a religious leader to say it's okay to use the Internet. Regardless of what we learn from research, we must always put it to the test of our own experience. This is the new awareness of people today. We are open to different messages, but we go with what is true for ourselves.

Waiting for academic approval is like waiting for a religious leader to say it's okay to use the Internet.

When I teach the new and radical ideas in my book *Children Are from Heaven,* people's resistance quickly melts. They begin to experience how to parent their kids with greater ease by improving communication and giving up the old methods of punishment. Even people who are initially resistant find themselves convinced after doing the role-playing exercises and directly experiencing the process. Those who haven't taken a workshop but have read the book are impressed when they put my ideas to the test and discover personally that they not only make sense, but that they work.

In teaching practical miracles, I have had the same experience. People naturally have doubts, but when they begin directly experiencing their new potential to recharge with positive energy and discharge stress, their resistance melts away. When it comes to creating practical miracles, it's hard to believe the process could be so simple and easy until you try.

The Times Are Changing

The times have truly changed. Living in harmony with the nine guiding principles is no longer so difficult. It is not only easy, but it immediately makes living easier. This is because mankind has already lived through their development. We are now capable of putting these principles into practice and making our dreams come true.

Many people are already living by some of the nine principles, but few live by all nine at once. Yet each of the nine principles for creating practical miracles is equally important. Men and women often experience limited success in life because they are missing the wisdom of just one principle they aren't implementing.

Each principle complements the eight others in order to create success. Without an integration of all nine, practical miracles cannot be sustained. To create lasting love, increasing success, and vibrant health, we need to incorporate all nine principles for creating practical miracles.

Without an integration of all nine principles, practical miracles cannot be sustained.

These distinct principles were acted out in a variety of ways, frequently showing up as fads and sometimes as revolutionary changes or shifts. A quick review of only a few of them points out how miraculous these times really are.

In the second half of the twentieth century, changes that would have taken hundreds of years to unfold occurred in a few months. The perfect fifties, the liberated sixties, the consciousness-raising seventies, the booming eighties and the high-tech nineties were all dramatically different. Now at last we arrive at the miraculous new millennium—a time when we can incorporate the best of each of these periods.

Seven-Year Growth Spurts

Each of the first seven principles was awakened, lived, and challenged by society during the last half century. Although we were just holding on for the ride, our consciousness was going through the final changes to appreciate and understand them fully.

In 1950 mankind began experiencing the opening of this growing awareness of the principles in seven distinct stages, each unfolding perfectly every seven years. With each unfolding, people made a radical shift in the way they attempted to live their lives.

Certainly not all society consciously participated in each of these changes, but every person was influenced by them according to his or her own particular needs. To review these shifts awakens us to our own direct experience of the different guiding principles for creating practical miracles.

To remember our personal experience of these principles, our struggles as well as happy attempts to master them, makes them more concrete. Although at the time we didn't recognize their magnitude, we can now look back and realize how much we really have changed.

**The possibility of rapid change is
one of greatest practical miracles.**

In each of these seven-year periods, the miraculous energy of each principle was released successively. During each seven-year growth spurt, our capacity to comprehend each of the principles evolved. It didn't matter whether we were actively participating with the energy or resisting it. We were all influenced by it, as our children are now and as their children will be.

Let's now review a few of the astonishing changes and developments of the last fifty years and explore how they directly relate to each of the first seven principles for creating practical miracles. By reviewing a few of the many significant changes in the last fifty years all at once, we can recognize how social change has become miraculously accelerated. This recognition awakens in you a more expanded awareness of the possibilities for making personal changes. Heightened awareness of the changes around us increases our personal capacity to create meaningful change.

1. Believe As If Miracles Are Possible.

Between 1950 and 1957, with World War II behind us, we experienced increasing optimism. Democracy had triumphed and people were confident they could make their dreams come true. Countries were coming together for the first time in history with the hope of world peace.

Positive thinking was everywhere. In 1952 Norman Vincent Peale, author of *The Power of Positive Thinking,* founded his center and began to share his uplifting and inspirational message with millions. For some, however, growing optimism quickly turned to arrogance. McCarthyism was in full swing. In the name of patriotism, an outrageous and shameful witch-hunt began. Suddenly "our way" was the best way. The government, like an overcontrolling parent, laid down the rules, and "the teens" rebelled. This "one way" thinking was soon to be challenged by the coming radical changes of the sixties.

Although family life in the fifties looked perfect on the surface, it wasn't. Problems existed but they were well hidden. Positive thinking, when taken to an extreme, turns to rigidity, denial, and selective vision. Young Elvis Presley was dubbed "Elvis the Pelvis" by conservatives, and his new way of dancing was censored on TV with cameras filming him only from the waist up.

In the fifties, we learned that positive is good but that we must also acknowledge what doesn't work as well. Those who do not recognize the need for change become stale. Maintaining the status quo is against life and results in a passionless existence. In the next seven years, this rigidity was transcended and replaced by a new sense of freedom by the sixties revolution.

2. Live As If You Are Free to Do What You Want.

Between 1956 and 1964, Elvis exploded and rock and roll was here to stay. The Baby Boomers began coming of age. The beat of change had literally picked up. Young people were dancing freely and speaking with open minds and open hearts. Change was in the air. We literally were moving to the beat of our own hearts. Our challenge during this period was to unlock the gates that held us back from being truly ourselves.

Old inhibitions and limitations were replaced by liberating ideals. In 1957 Russia launched *Sputnik* and the Space Age began. In 1960 John Kennedy, the second-youngest president in U.S. history, was elected and proceeded to set his sights on the moon. Astronauts Alan Shepard, Virgil Grissom, and John Glenn, along with NASA, set Kennedy's lofty plans in motion. What were once dreams now were becoming a reality.

In 1963, at a civil rights rally in Washington, D.C., Martin Luther King Jr., in front of two hundred thousand activists, delivered his historic and inspiring "I Have a Dream" message, and the human rights movement, the changing tide of increasing freedom, was raised to new heights.

Yet, even increasing freedom can have a chaotic and sometimes destructive side. In 1965 six days of riots in the Watts section of Los Angeles shook the nation. A new awareness of minority rights gave rise to a demand for real freedom and equality. Years of pain from abuse were suddenly unleashed. Racial violence broke out in a number of major U.S. cities. On the other side of the world, in South Africa, Nelson Mandela spoke out for freedom and was sentenced to life in prison for doing so.

The publication of Betty Friedan's landmark book *The Feminine Mystique* ushered in a wave of feminism that ignited controversy and heated discussions between the sexes. In 1966 the National Organization for Women was founded, and our journey toward equality between men and women had begun. Helen Gurley Brown took over *Cosmopolitan* magazine and provided an ongoing venue for women looking to redefine themselves and release outdated, limiting stereotypes. In the ensuing years, feminist Gloria Steinem founded *Ms.* magazine and further inspired women to fight for their rights.

Conventional ways and traditions were now being challenged on every front. By defying authority, James Dean, the "rebel without a cause," became the role model for American youth. Freedom was on the rise. During this time, we learned that following our hearts was not necessarily the same as acting on our every whim. Just doing the opposite of what others want us to do is not necessarily freedom.

Unless we know what is really important to us, doing whatever we want can make us superficial and disconnected from what is really true or important. This insight opened the door to going deeper within ourselves. We quickly awakened to our deepest and primary need in life, the need to love and to do what we love.

3. Learn As If You Are a Beginner.

Between 1964 and 1971, with new innocence and openness the love generation sprung into being. In 1964 Ed Sullivan introduced Americans to "four talented young men from Liverpool." To the frenzied squeals and screams of adoring female fans, the Beatles ushered in a new and glorious time of innocence, music, laughter, and love. "I Want to Hold Your Hand" soared to the top of the charts. "All you need is love" is a theme that endures.

While the young were committed to love and following their hearts, on the home front our government was fighting a war against communism to "make the world safe for democracy." Many young people took a stand against violence and formed the peace movement. On campuses around the country, young people, speaking their minds, protested our involvement in Vietnam, called for the immediate withdrawal of troops, and demanded that the government be accountable for its mistake.

The young people wanted to rewrite the rules. During this period, our challenge was to break free of limiting traditions and find a better way to learn from our past and not repeat the same mistakes. We then went on to protest and demand change.

In addition to envisioning world peace, public awareness shifted to the health of our planet. April 22, 1970, marked the first Earth Day. Cleaning up toxic pollution, protecting wildlife, and preserving our natural resources for future generations became a critical concern. The green movement demanded that government and big business be accountable for wasting and abusing our natural resources.

We opened our minds and hearts in other ways as well. We, like any young teenagers, suddenly knew everything and our parents knew nothing. No one over thirty was to be trusted. We wanted more than the past could give us. We wanted to start over and do things differently.

Many young people became interested in consciousness expansion to find inner happiness. In 1968 the Beatles went to India to learn from the Maharishi, who taught transcendental meditation, or TM. Meditation became an option for millions who wanted to get high without taking drugs. A variety of Eastern gurus and teachers began traveling to the West.

For many, the "New Age" had officially started once we began turning inward to seek change. While millions learned to meditate or practice yoga, others experimented with recreational drugs. They turned on and dropped out. "Free love" was our motto and the peace sign our symbol. Everyone wanted to do his or her own thing. With flower power, hippies, demonstrators, and draft dodgers, the psychedelic sixties was a colorful and tumultuous time. With many getting high in a variety of ways, life was both "far out" and "groovy."

Young men threw away their watches, grew out their hair, and hit the road on their new Harleys. In 1969 the movie *Easy Rider*, starring Peter Fonda, Dennis Hopper, and a young actor named Jack Nicholson, captured the imagination of the young everywhere. This was clearly a time of increasing freedom and new beginnings.

In the same year, women began leaving their husbands. No-fault divorce legislation was passed in 1969, and in twelve months, divorce statistics rose from 10 to 50 percent, maintaining that same level until the end of the twentieth century. People wanted happiness and real love, and they were going to find it even if it meant changing partners.

The untamed and unbridled freedom of this stage was corrected during the next period of increasing realism. The idealism of this stage was quickly replaced by an increased awareness of the harsh realities of pain and suffering that come from injustice. It was fine to be idealistic, but bills had to be paid and children needed to be fed.

4. Love As If for the First Time.

Between 1971 and 1978, the "me generation" appeared. As the Baby Boomers became parents themselves, they were forced to face the financial obligations of earning a living and raising a family. People pulled back from getting high on drugs and sought to be more responsible. Long hair was out and retirement funds were in.

It was a time to work hard and to play hard. Given this more grounded reality, women and men realized they needed to care for themselves before they could give more to others. To balance this sobering awareness, we were determined to lighten up as well.

Disco was in. John Travolta ignited the passions of boundless moviegoers in *Saturday Night Fever,* and the fever was contagious. The idealistic free love of the sixties was quickly reduced to casual encounters. People began to experiment with sex, expecting no commitment so they couldn't get hurt. Love had to be light and fun as well as realistic.

But not everyone was happy. Despite the close of the Vietnam War in 1975, the many years of protest had taken a toll on the American psyche. Our returning soldiers were greeted by a less than friendly welcome and struggled to rebuild their lives after experiencing the horrors and devastation of war. It would take years until the Vietnam War Memorial in Washington, D.C., was built and the veterans received the recognition they deserved.

It was a time of peace, but the country needed to heal. Our challenge was to acknowledge injustice but seek forgiveness as well. Mistrust was in the air with the exposure of Watergate and other incidents of government corruption. In 1974 Richard Nixon resigned; Gerald Ford became president, and, soon after, Nixon was pardoned. In 1977, after Jimmy Carter became president, he pardoned the Vietnam draft dodgers. In 1979 Anwar el-Sadat of Egypt and Menachem Begin of Israel signed a historic plan for peace in the Middle East. With increasing accountability for our mistakes, a new level of forgiveness was required to heal our wounds.

Our sense of obligation increased as well. In the financial venue, we suddenly became aware of our debts and accountabilities. Interest rates skyrocketed, and the economy plummeted. Empty pocketbooks and skepticism stifled our newfound freedom.

In a variety of ways we were experiencing the limits of liberation. Once again we confronted the hard fact that life had boundaries. We couldn't just give freely; we had to see to our own needs first. We were running on empty in our personal lives, and soon our cars would mirror us. Suddenly there was an energy shortage. Not only our personal resources, but the earth's resources, were limited. We had plenty of time to reflect on our needs as we waited in long lines to fill our tanks.

Pop psychology molded the intellectual ideas of Freud, Jung, and others into a form that could benefit and be easily understood by the general public. More and more people began participating in self-help and "encounter" groups. Therapy was no longer a luxury for the rich or something to be kept secret. The desire for self-improvement became an acceptable, even an admirable, aspiration. California-based transformational seminars caught the public's attention and went on the road.

Alcoholics Anonymous, founded in the thirties, thrived, and other more recently formed twelve-step groups flourished. Millions of men and women across the land literally sobered up to face life's challenges more successfully. This was a time to realize not just what we had been doing to others, but to ourselves as well. With the curtain of denial pulled back, people were willing and able to change.

Having focused on themselves for this period, the Baby Boomers were now ready to explore giving from a sense of self-sufficiency and autonomy. This grounded awareness and confidence set the stage for the next period of unprecedented economic growth, investment, and expansion.

5. Give As If You Already Have What You Need.

Between 1978 and 1985, we shifted into the booming eighties. In 1980 Ronald Reagan rode in on a white horse to save the day. The timing was perfect. On the day of his inauguration, the Iran hostage crisis ended, and we could finally relax. The impending doom of previous years was now balanced by a more tempered but still romantic sense of abundance.

Reagan was a seasoned actor and played the role of president flawlessly. The state of the union never looked brighter than after he spoke. With this attitudinal shift, our country began to blossom in many respects. Although America still had problems, we knew everything would be fine because our president always looked so happy and at ease. Interest rates went down and the economy flourished. People felt more and more secure about investing their earnings in the soaring stock market.

Our president radiated confidence. When we saw him coming off Air Force One with a friendly wave to the camera, we knew he was off to take an afternoon stroll in the garden with Nancy, followed by a well-deserved nap. If he could stop and smell the roses, then so could we. Reaganomics assured us we could have it all. While business was booming, our government was sinking into a deep well of debt.

Given more equal opportunities than ever before in history, women were making inroads everywhere. Not only did they have access to higher-paying jobs, they also assumed career roles formerly reserved for men, who nevertheless persisted in defending their turf. Sandra Day O'Connor was the first woman appointed to the Supreme Court. Margaret Thatcher led Great Britain as its prime minister. Sally Ride became the first woman astronaut.

Our increasing abundance was indeed a great relief from the shortages of the past, but it also created new problems. Government spending was reflected in the private sphere. We, too, started drowning in debt from high living on credit and risky investments. We were obsessed with capital gains and what we could purchase with our new credit cards. Madonna captured this mood perfectly in her song *Material Girl*.

For many, money had become a new god to be worshiped. Through appeasing this god with hard work and sacrifice, you could earn the blessings of happiness, love, good fortune, and fulfillment. Although millions were making easy or fast money in the stock market, the levels of personal stress and distress increased proportionately.

Even while the stock market soared, homelessness was on the rise. Reagan, who clearly recognized our potential to make our dreams come true, was also completely unaware that some of us needed more help than others. Indifference and sometimes hostility to the poor are common limitations of those who are not.

Social programs to aid the mentally ill were cut, and the most helpless elements of our society were tossed out into streets to fend for themselves. Though some could meet this challenge, most could not. Living in the streets generally made matters worse. Like a line of dominoes collapsing tile by tile, homelessness magnified the social problem of drug abuse.

To escape the pain of living in poverty, street people turned to drugs, and, once addicted, became pushers. With an increase in drug availability, crime statistics rose sharply. Our teens began to reject their parents' values even more dramatically. Never before had society experienced so much domestic violence. On the one hand we were encouraged to "just do it," and on the other we were told to "just say no."

For those who prospered and lived the "good life," looming debt became a new source of enormous stress. With the cost of living on the rise, we had to work longer hours to pay our bills. For women who at first had relished their new opportunities to climb the ladder of success, staying at home was no longer an option. Two incomes were a necessity for couples if they wished to maintain their new lifestyle. We were now suffering the consequences and pressures that result from instant gratification and living beyond our means. Getting what you want is worthless if you don't have the time to enjoy it. Even as money became more available, we experienced a shortage of time and an increase in debt.

During this period of radical change, men and women were motivated to have it all and to do it all. While our healthy optimism had reached new heights, it had also revealed new limitations and challenges. Although increased freedom empowers us, it also means we must make more choices. More choices lead to greater stress and distress. Our priorities were work and success, but they had a price. "Overwhelmed" and "stressed out" became our buzzwords.

In the next seven years, this extraordinary pressure to do it all and to have it all would be relieved greatly. To reduce stress, society began focusing on what was really important, and it wasn't money. Society now had a chance to come back home and recognize its values and responsibilities.

In 1982 there was not a dry eye in the theaters as Steven Spielberg's adorable E.T. withered away on his bed while longing to phone home. With these immortal words, "phone home," the age of communication was onto a new frontier. This shift opened a new window of accelerated growth and unlimited creativity that history never has before encountered.

6. Work As If Money Doesn't Matter.

Between 1985 and 1992, our values shifted from money, and social issues became more important. As a result, we moved into a creative period of unprecedented growth. Once Apple Computers and later IBM launched the first series of desktop personal computers, the world would never be the same. With unprecedented speed, the infant high-tech industry would miraculously grow to global domination of all other industries. Every fiber of virtually every society in the world has been transformed by the birth of personal computers.

Creativity and motivation surged as people were propelled into this new world of endless possibilities. Accelerated change was occurring everywhere. Relations with Russia had never been better. In 1985 Reagan met with Mikhail Gorbachev in a historic summit; tensions between the superpowers seemed to have dissolved. We were confronting a "New World Order," and to be successful, we had to be open to change and eager to learn to use the new technology.

In 1987 the antidepressant drug Prozac was introduced and quickly embraced by millions. Never before had so many people been given the opportunity to experience the benefits as well as the limitations of freedom and money. With the direct experience of what more money brings, we began to realize that its seductive promise of fulfillment was partly an illusion. We learned that money cannot make us happy unless we are already happy. While the homeless were addicted to drugs to avoid the pain of poverty, the more affluent became dependent on psychological medications to deal with the depression and disappointment that often comes with having more.

The election of George Bush in 1988 ushered in a "kinder and gentler" era. Within the next few years, the Berlin Wall came down; the Dalai Lama won the Nobel Peace Prize; Nelson Mandela was freed from prison in South Africa; Lech Wałesa became the president of a free Poland. As our priorities began to change, respect for human rights came to prominence.

In 1989 this new surge of openness to change was felt by Chinese youths at Tiananmen Square, but their efforts were suppressed by the Chinese military. Though the young people were expressing their need for human rights, the government was slow to get their message.

In 1989 another tragedy took place, once again shifting society toward greater responsibility: the *Exxon Valdez* oil spill in Alaska. Although a costly disaster for our precious environment, it brought home the point that it is big business's responsibility to clean up its mistakes and to protect the environment.

Society was exploring and recognizing new and old values. Suddenly the "silent moral majority" spoke up for family values, and the government started spending more money on social programs. On the political right, a woman's right to an abortion was being seriously challenged, and on the political left, liberals were beginning to support alternative lifestyles. By the 1990s, gay pride celebrations appeared not only in San Francisco and New York but in most major U.S. cities, as well as other countries around the globe. Although many people did not understand the need for alternative lifestyles, they were still willing to respect human rights.

While some worried that we were declining into a period of decadence, others felt that by respecting human rights we were becoming more socially responsible. Society as a whole began to admire integrity, not just the shine of gold. Our values were changing. This shift toward greater respect for others' values ushered in a time of incredible efficiency and accelerated growth.

The Persian Gulf War of 1991 was the most televised military conflict in history. CNN made its debut and introduced around-the-clock news coverage and satisfied our new insatiable thirst for information. While missiles were landing, the whole world watched. That same year, apartheid laws were repealed in South Africa and sanctions against the country were lifted. On the heels of the historic breakup of the Soviet Union, Boris Yeltsin became the first freely elected president of Russia. He formally proclaimed the end of the Cold War in 1992.

As values changed, we shifted away from the tensions of the Cold War and slipped into the warmth of a hot bath. It was time to relax and enjoy what we had. Suddenly men and women stopped rejecting each other and started wanting peace. Throughout history, we had always lived in different worlds. Now we wanted to live together in love and passion on earth. Understanding, validation, and communication were the means to bridge the gulf between men and women. Similarly, the whole world began to relax and connect as new technology dramatically improved and accelerated our ability to communicate.

7. Relax As If Everything Will Be Okay.

From 1992 to 1999, "communication" became the new buzzword and was considered to be the solution to all problems—at work, at home, in relationships, even with God. High tech reached an even higher level of communication with the invention of the Internet, which had connected the entire globe. With this one change, the analog world went digital. By means of more efficient communication of images and information, the opportunities for change and growth became infinitely faster. During this period, people started making their dreams come true.

Relationships and romance became a booming industry, with experts, programs, and seminars promising to improve communication between the sexes. Businesses hired consultants to inspire better communications in order to improve working conditions. With so many job opportunities, companies realized that to retain their employees they needed to listen to their needs.

My book *Men Are from Mars, Women Are from Venus,* a guide for improving communication, became the number one bestselling book of the decade. After the Senate hearings of Clarence Thomas and Anita Hill, diversity trainings turned up everywhere to stop sexual harassment in the workplace.

People wanted to talk about everything. "Let's talk about it" became the new option to fighting. Parents began teaching their children to "use your words" instead of hitting. Talk shows conquered TV, and gossip newspapers and magazines flourished. From President Clinton's sex life to Oprah's current diet to the infidelities of the British royal family, anything that provided more communication was gobbled up.

By taking spiritual ideas into the living rooms of millions, *Touched by an Angel* became one of television's most popular shows. *Unsolved Mysteries, X-Files,* and other TV specials featuring strange and wondrous occurrences began popping up. Stories of near-death experiences and visions of the world beyond were reported along with such practical miracles as the sudden spiritual healing of serious physical conditions.

Dramatic hurricanes, tornadoes, weather changes, and earthquakes significantly increased. More natural disasters occurred in the nineties than in the previous hundred years. Even earth changes were speeding up. With each disaster, the awesome forces of nature once again humbled mankind. This awakened in us a need for God. As a result, survivors came together and turned to God for help. Hundreds of millions of people were affected by these tragedies. There were probably more prayers uttered during this period than ever before in history.

For those who were more conservative in nature, there was a resurgent interest in religion. The churches and temples began attracting more worshipers. Those who were more liberal sought spiritual fulfillment in the skyrocketing personal-growth movement. During this time, spiritual books and self-help manuals topped the bestseller lists.

Though people thought it was impossible, stock prices continued to go up. Microsoft's Bill Gates became a billionaire practically overnight. In the early nineties, his three billion dollars made him the richest man in the world. Within a few more years, he was worth eighty billion!

Almost everyone began investing, and mutual funds consistently made more money every year. Those who invested in high-tech stocks made millions of dollars. As the Internet began to connect the whole world, people became even more optimistic about its potential. For the first time, serious investors bought stock even in companies that lost money. Companies that had yet to realize their potential were being purchased for billions of dollars.

While many people were going online and investing in the Internet, others were investing in their relationships and beginning to heal the wounds of divorce and broken families. In the last year of the twentieth century, for the first time since 1969, the consistent 50 percent divorce rate went down by 20 percent.

While some experienced increasing success and love, others began exploring and developing their inner potential. The human potential movement rose to even higher levels of popularity. At the same time, we were deep into a health-care crisis. People were clearly not getting the care they required. They began letting go of their dependence on traditional doctors and started looking for alternative treatments.

While some were disillusioned with medical care, others were spiritually disillusioned. They had picked the "higher path" but were still not experiencing many of the practical perks in life that people of lesser faith enjoyed. It didn't seem fair that really good people could become sick with cancer, lose money, or get divorced. Suddenly it appeared that having faith, doing good, forgiving, and being forgiven were not enough to reap life's bounty.

If God was listening to their prayers, then how could these awful things have happened? Some felt betrayed by God, while others remained open but rejected God's message as it was given to them by others. They turned elsewhere to find their answers. As a result, throughout the nineties, alternative forms of self-development became increasingly popular.

For a major segment of the nineties religious attendance continued to go up. Suddenly, spiritual books were regularly seen on the bestseller lists. It seemed everyone was reading about the legendary miraculous powers of ancient days. The Harry Potter books began selling out and were being read not just by children but by adults as well.

In 1998 Oprah started "Change Your Life TV" and featured at the end of each show a special segment titled "Return to Spirit." There was also a revival of interest in Eastern spiritualities. Meditation and yoga were in once again. Many millions became interested in the practical benefits of Buddhism as taught by exiled Tibetan monks.

In 1998, when Viagra came on the market, millions of men rushed to take it to cure sexual impotence. The possibility of a quick fix prompted them to acknowledge a problem that had plagued men throughout history.

As a man aged beyond forty, or after having been married for several years, he often lost his sexual desire. Rather than being regarded as a problem to overcome, his sudden disinterest in sex was mistakenly concluded to be the natural outcome of getting old. He would simply accept it instead of recognize it to be a health problem that could be cured by dietary adjustments, romantic skills, and better communication.

Besides making money there is no other arena of a man's life in which he feels more pressure to perform than making love. Once Viagra was readily available, and with no pressure to perform, waning sex drives began to revive.

This last decade of the twentieth century awakened us to the real possibility of making our dreams come true in all areas of life. At the movies, where dreams are often depicted as possible, sales dramatically increased. Stars went from making five million dollars a picture to twenty million. Instead of grossing ten to twenty million, successful films grossed hundreds of millions. Disney Studios, which has traditionally made movies of fairy tales and dreams coming true, flourished. For the first time since the early days of making movies, a new Hollywood movie studio, DreamWorks, was founded.

Women who had fought for feminism following the promise and dream that you could have it all realized something was still missing in their lives. Some were disillusioned with feminism; others bravely pushed on. Progress was made on both fronts. Employers allowed flexible work hours. Many women postponed having babies or took time off from their careers to follow their hearts and be with their children. They realized they could have it all but not necessarily all at the same time.

Growing with the Rich and Famous

With the invention of television, the lives of the famous became part of the home life of everyone. As the beautiful, gifted, rich, powerful, or celebrated people endured their dramatic and often bigger-than-life trials and tests, we endured their ordeals with them. The problems of our leaders and stars became our own problems. Along with them, we learned from their mistakes and losses.

Like it or not, it is through television that the world has become a global family. We have all shared the same friends, tears, and jokes each night. Although television can certainly become an addiction and clearly some programming is inappropriate for children, the invention and development of television has helped bring mankind together.

**Through television the world
has become a global family.**

Through this medium, along with movies, people of all cultures can and do experience the common thread that is within everyone, regardless of race, sex, religion, or status in life. Television has enabled society to connect easily with the rapid changes of the world. As we have become increasingly aware of change, the possibilities for creating change in our own lives has dramatically increased. The communication of ideas and pictures through TV has awakened mankind to the possibilities within every person.

A Vision of Clinton's Greatness

Even political turmoil has served to increase awareness. With the attack on President Clinton in the nineties, everyone was discussing sex and fidelity. Although this subject needed to be aired, the whole scandal served another purpose as well. Bill Clinton showed the world that even a president is not perfect, and the world forgave him his indiscretions. Although probing into his private life was a violation and, practically speaking, a huge waste of his time and ours, it did serve a greater purpose. For the age of miracles to occur, people needed to have their heroes lovingly dethroned. Not only did the voters forgive him, but his wife and family stood by him as well.

It is disempowering to consider another as "better than you" or somehow above you. As long as we treat other humans as gods, or supermen and superwomen, then we cannot recognize that God lives within each person and that we all have equal access to God's grace.

Clinton has been the most human of all our presidents—a vulnerable collection of virtue and vice. Right from the start, he cried a "real" tear at his inauguration, and displayed true heartfelt feeling. He has never claimed to be above the common man. He grew up in poverty and truly cares for the needy and poor. Regardless of our political convictions, we recognize he is a human, and we all respect him for his noble efforts to make the world a better place. We forgive his mistakes and don't see him as less because of them. To his many supporters, he remains a "real" human who is "really" great.

When we can see him as great *and* as a human capable of making mistakes, then we are released from the false notion that we have to be perfect in order to be great as well. We are liberated from the limiting notion that others can be great but we cannot. We all have greatness within, regardless of how many mistakes we have made. Just as we have forgiven Clinton, so we can forgive ourselves. What separates mediocrity from greatness is our ability to recognize our mistakes with forgiveness and then learn from them. This is one of the many gifts Bill Clinton gave to his country and the world.

The Real Magic of Oprah

Every day 30 million viewers around the world eagerly watch Oprah humbly step down from the golden pedestal of power, glamour, fame, and wealth. As she so honestly and courageously shares her trials and tribulations, viewers feel empowered with the knowledge that she can relate to their pain. She, too, is not above making mistakes or feeling hurt. She, too, struggles with issues involving her body, relationships, and work.

When she claims you can change your life, it means something because she has done it and continues to do it. She is not an especially lucky person who has been spared the setbacks, pain, and disappointments we all experience. She doesn't separate herself from her audience, yet sets an example of how you can return to spirit and create practical miracles in your own life. As she continues to learn and grow, so does her audience. If she can do it, then we feel we can do it as well.

Oprah is a good example of the new teacher in this age of miracles—someone willing to share her vulnerabilities as well as proudly acknowledging and demonstrating her strengths and accomplishments. When our heroes are just like us, we are free to find the real hero within ourselves.

The Death of Fairy Tales

In 1992 Princess Diana and Prince Charles decided to separate; four years later they were divorced. A year after the divorce, Diana was tragically killed in a car accident. Never before has there been so much global interest in a relationship. This couple represented the hopes and dreams of every person. Their marriage ceremony was the perfect fairy-tale wedding, which the whole world watched on TV. The Prince and Princess had everything one could hope for to be happy, and yet they weren't.

Each day the world tuned in to their next mishap as if it were a daily soap opera—except their life tribulations were real.

Diana was beautiful, charismatic, charming, glamorous, loving, playful, and, to top that, she was married to a dashing, powerful, intelligent, and handsome prince. In spite of all that, his romantic attention quickly waned, and she was often miserable.

The consistent truth Diana demonstrated is that having it all means nothing when it came to being happy or being loved in a relationship. Many people already sensed that you can't buy happiness, but they had no proof. Diana's sad life and tragic death makes this concept real for people. Unless you really "have everything," you cannot honestly know that having more doesn't make you happy. The truth that the rich and privileged were not necessarily more fulfilled was no longer just a notion but an established fact.

Unless you really have everything, you cannot honestly know that having more doesn't make you happy.

Diana's suffering only made people love her more. Her life and marriage taught the world that keeping a stiff upper lip and looking good was not enough. Diana had failed in her life to be happy and find love, but her fans loved her unconditionally. This unconditional love was healing for all of us. It meant if ordinary people also failed, they, too, were still loveable. This was one of Diana's great gifts to the world.

Princess Diana taught the world that keeping a stiff upper lip and looking good was not enough.

The ability to love ourselves, even though we are not perfect, comes from recognizing that others are not perfect, but still loveable. What made Diana unique was her ongoing search for fulfillment. It must have taken enormous courage to follow her heart and leave the royal family. What a shocking change for a Princess of Wales to forsake the possibility of becoming the Queen of England.

Princess Diana represented the new woman of the nineties who was unwilling to settle for a relationship without real love and romance. If she couldn't find love, then she was willing to give it all up and start over. As a result, people were encouraged to follow their hearts as well. If Diana could make her needs more important than trying to conform to the royal traditions of the past, then we could also shed our old tendencies to sacrifice too much and instead begin to follow our hearts.

The Dethroning of Idols

The dethroning of the "great" or the "idols" of the masses in the last days of the twentieth century served to liberate our consciousness and awaken our capacity to experience the new practical power of our own inner greatness.

8. Talk to God As If You Are Being Heard.

The years from 1999 to 2006 will complete this fifty-six-year cycle of awakening to our new inner potential to create practical miracles. This step will be done especially with God's help. In 1999 and 2000, instead of doom as predicted by Y2K scares, we continued to experience unprecedented growth and optimism. This growth will only continue as people begin to access their new power to create lasting love, increasing success, and vibrant health. There will certainly be ups and downs, but the growth that results will be unprecedented in history.

9. Feast As If You Can Have Whatever You Want.

The years from 2006 to 2013 will begin a new cycle and a new beginning for the world. With the radical advances in both outer and inner technology, all people will have access to greater education, flexible work hours, and a multitude of opportunities to make their dreams come true.

Global values will adjust to incorporate our more advanced consciousness that is capable of creating practical miracles. The world that we have all dreamed of for ourselves and our loved ones will no longer be a lofty ideal but instead a practical reality.

Problems will continue as they always have, but, instead of creating conflict and corruption, they will inspire greater cooperation, compassion, equality, and fairness throughout the world. Through facing our new challenges together, we will express and sustain a new power that humanity has only glimpsed in the past. People will be free to write their own story in life and to develop the many gifts within, which they were born to develop and share.

Ancient Wisdom and Common Sense

During each of the past seven-year growth spurts, mankind began learning and putting together the ancient wisdom of the ages. Truths that in the past only the most enlightened and educated could hope to comprehend were now becoming matters of direct experience and common sense. In these last fifty years, the fruit of our consciousness ripened, and we were ready to begin reevaluating everything we ever believed or didn't believe, and to experience for ourselves what was true.

With just a little hard work or deliberate effort we can now make things happen that were never believed possible. We can begin to understand the answers to questions that we have long carried deep within our hearts. This is the time when all our prayers can be answered and all our dreams can come true. The possibility is there, but it is up to us, using our new capacity, to do it.

6

A LIFE FREE FROM BURDEN

Life is not a burden when you feel confident and self-sufficient. With the direct experience of your inner power to create miracles, you will find a reservoir of inner strength. As you use this strength, your power to create practical miracles will increase. If we are confident and life presents us with big problems, they are no longer huge burdens. Instead, big problems become big challenges that pull forth more of your greatness.

When a problem causes us to feel burdened or causes us to close our hearts, it is a signal that we have disconnected from our true power. It is a signal to focus on reconnecting to our inner power before trying to make changes in the outer world. It is a time to focus on forgiving and letting go, so that you can come into present time and make the best of a situation. When we are connected in present time to our true selves, then we always feel some peace, joy, confidence, or love. These positive feelings always will begin to come up when we let go of the past and focus on what we can do now to create a better future. When we come back to ourselves in present time by letting go of past pain, we begin to experience increasing degrees of the peace, joy, confidence, and love that are always in our hearts.

When life becomes an emotional disturbance and we are unable to move swiftly through our feelings and release our pain, it is a sign to forget about the problem at hand temporarily and solve the most important problem. We must first remove the block within ourselves and re-experience our power to generate an authentic positive attitude that reflects our true self and power. Most of the time when we experience emotional distress, we have just temporarily forgotten that we have the power to grow from any circumstance.

Overdependence in Relationships

Whenever our disappointments block our love, trust, and appreciation for our partner, it is a sign that we have become too dependent. Overdependence is an old habit that now can be quickly released as you begin to awaken your inner potential to be happy and loving. By learning to follow your heart and do what you love more of the time, you automatically will be less dependent on your partner. With this greater self-sufficiency, you will be able to forgive more easily and learn to love as if for the first time This is one of the practical miracles that you will be experiencing every day.

Without this power it always seems as if our partner, our economic condition, or some outer circumstance is responsible for our misery or upset. The good news is that we are always responsible for how we feel. We certainly can affect others with our attitude and actions, but we cannot fully control the outer world. We can, however, control our inner world. Every person now can begin to tap into his or her inner potential to generate loving and trusting feelings.

Hurricane and the Blessings of Forgiveness

This message of forgiveness is wonderfully exemplified in the life story of an undefeated world-champion boxer named Rubin "Hurricane" Carter. His inspirational true story is depicted in a movie based on his life, entitled *Hurricane*. He was a victim of racial discrimination and was unjustly imprisoned for most of his life. During a series of disappointments and challenges, he eventually was able to find inner peace through forgiveness while still in prison. The movie climaxes with the following realization and statement, while still imprisoned: "My hate put me in this prison and love has set me free."

This courageous man was able to forgive the most horrible discrimination, injustice, humiliation, and abuse, yet eventually found peace and felt love in his heart for the people who had so unjustly mistreated him. Just as Christ was able to forgive his tormentors, Hurricane, the undefeated boxer, was able to find forgiveness in his heart.

Hurricane had found his freedom while living in prison. His miracle was to be free from the hate that he said had ruled his life. His second miracle was to be released from prison. He first set himself free. Then, finally, the truth of his innocence was revealed, and he was released from prison.

First his inner freedom and then his outer freedom were the blessings of forgiveness. By finding forgiveness in his heart, his attempts to change the outer world could be more successful. By changing our inner attitude regarding the world, the outer world begins to reflect back our inner state and changes in some way. Although we never really have the power to control others, we can maximize our influence.

When we forgive an injustice, we begin to attract more justice. When we don't forgive, we tend to attract more injustice. Certainly this injustice is never our fault, but somehow we are attracted to the same kinds of situations when we don't forgive. As we learn to forgive, we tend to attract better situations. Even when we are putting forth our most positive selves, we still may not get the justice we deserve, but we will get more.

When Hurricane forgave others for their mistakes, the perpetrators of this abuse could begin to see the injustice of their actions. Although he was a victim, and thus never in any way responsible for the prejudice against him, he overcame his plight through forgiveness. As a result, his power to create change in the outer world increased as well. It is the courage and strength of people like Hurricane that has helped move and prepare mankind for this new age.

Hurricane's transformation is an example of the kind of miracles that are possible today. For thousands of years, spiritual traditions have taught us to accept the limitations of the world and to find freedom and love within ourselves. For spiritual aspirants in the West, life was a process to endure with love and charity and the reward would be in heaven. For spiritual seekers in the East, by achieving a positive inner state of equanimity and compassion, one hoped to attain *moksha,* enlightenment, or nirvana. Each is a different name for an exalted state, free of suffering.

These limited messages were completely appropriate for the people at that time because that is all they could possibly hope to attain. Most people were not yet ready to reach their higher potential. Now we are ready and can create a heaven on earth and live in it free from all suffering.

Today, changing your inner state is much easier and faster than ever before. With our new abilities, we quickly can learn to change our inner state and begin focusing more on creating the miracle of change in the outer world. We no longer have to wait for that day when the outer world will change. It is now time for us to follow Hurricane Carter's example and begin doing it. Fortunately, this change is now much faster and easier.

Instant Karma

John Lennon first popularized this notion of fast change in his song "Instant Karma." The basic idea is the world immediately mirrors your inner state. Though this was not everyone's experience, it was his. Since he was very aware of his inner world of feelings, he could express his unique creative genius. Since he was so aware of his inner world, he realized that in every moment, in some way, the outer world reflected back his inner state. This is actually true for everyone, but many are just not aware of their inner state.

The principle of instant karma is that if you are feeling really good inside, then "instantly" the people you interact with tend to make you feel really good. If you are anxious and in a hurry, then the grocery line you pick is always the slowest line and you feel even more in a hurry. If you are angry, then people do things to make you angrier. If you feel like a victim, then people do things to make you feel more like a victim. On the other hand, if you begin to let go of your anger, people begin to let go of theirs.

Instant karma means that what you put out is what you get back—instantly. It implies that the whole process is speeded up. The world mirrors you right now. The traditional Hindu notion of Karma or the Christian notion of "you reap what you sow" acknowledges that what you get is what you have put out in your past. If you plant corn, then you get corn. If you don't plant corn, then you don't get corn. While this was an advanced teaching thousands of years ago, most ten-year-olds today can completely understand it.

The updated version of karma is a little more complicated, but it is still easy to get. You still have to plant corn to get corn, but regardless of your past, you are not blocked from planting the corn. In the old model, if you were bad in a past life, you didn't get the right to plant corn in the next life. In a sense, you had to be punished until you were worthy of getting another chance.

Instant karma means that in every moment, whatever you are putting out, it will begin coming back to you. In any moment, if you are aware of what you are putting out, you can choose to create a new result. In any moment, regardless of your past, you can plant corn and soon reap a delicious golden crop of corn. You don't have to spend a lifetime or endure a jail sentence, suffering for your crimes.

For simplicity, let's extend this analogy of planting corn. In the past, if one were hungry and didn't have corn, one mistakenly concluded that one was unworthy and "less than others" who had corn. It was as if the wealthy corn eaters were somehow better people and thus more worthy of God's grace and bounty. To be without corn meant one was either being punished by God or just further away from God's favor. This wasn't true then and it's not true now. Although this is a simple concept to understand today, people in the past just could not get it. They were still struggling just to understand the ABCs of cause and effect.

A Brief History of Karma

Good begets good and bad begets bad was a new idea five thousand years ago. In ancient Egypt and Samaria, rather than feeling directly responsible for what happens, people believed that they were constantly under the attack of demons and bad spirits. Protection from these negative energies was obtained by pleasing their gods.

Gradually, mankind evolved and realized that one's own thoughts and actions had more to do with the results that occurred in one's life. This was simultaneous with the idea that there was one God within all the lesser gods and that one God was also within us. This shift supported a greater awareness of our personal responsibility for the results we get in life. By finding God within ourselves, we could access the power to create miracles.

When people finally got the notion of karma, or cause and effect, then the next idea was forgiveness. Society has struggled with this idea for the last two thousand years. It was difficult because it seemed to contradict the laws of karma or the ideas of cause and effect, which demanded an eye for an eye. As we are finally capable of understanding forgiveness, the door has opened to create miracles.

Karma and Punishment

Every action has a consequence, but at the same time, no one ever deserves punishment. One of the practical implications of forgiveness is the letting go of our need to punish. If someone is an unsafe driver, then the forgiving consequence is that they lose their driver's license until he or she can learn and prove to be a safe driver. Loving forgiveness does not give others permission to abuse us, but instead frees us to correct a situation with love and the intent to nurture, rather than to hurt back or punish.

As a practical benefit to us, forgiveness of others frees us from holding on to the pain that another has caused us. When the driver's license is taken away, this is not punishment but a protection of others until they learn to drive. Giving up punishment frees us and society to rehabilitate the offender rather than make the problem worse.

When we respond to the mistakes and the bad actions of others with the intent to punish, deprive, get even, or make someone feel guilty, it not only hurts them, but it locks us into the past as well. It serves no healthy purpose. To justify our willful intent to cause pain to another after punishing someone, we magnify and sustain the pain they caused us instead of letting it go.

Our justification of punishment could sound like this: "They deserve terrible punishment because their actions will keep me from ever being happy. They must pay the price and compensate me for my pain. They have no right to be happy when I am in such pain because of what they did to me."

By this statement to justify our punishing actions and attitudes, we are affirming our powerlessness to create a better life. This punishing attitude is a no-win situation. We lose and the perpetrator loses as well. It is very difficult to let go of our past and be fulfilled in the present when we punish or even want to punish others.

To forgive is to release the offender from any debt to us. When we forgive them, they win and we win. By letting it go, we are then free to be in the moment and start again to make the best of what happened and to move on. To focus on what was lost or the pain that was caused, we are forced to live once again in the past. It is great to remember the past and learn from it, but holding on to the past limits our power to create our future. By holding on, you are allowing someone else to continue creating your future.

By holding on to the pain of the past, we are allowing someone else to continue creating our future.

If we believe others deserve punishment, then we believe we deserve punishment, and as a result, we will continue to punish ourselves consciously or subconsciously for the mistakes we have made. Many good and loving people hold themselves back in life and don't experience their true power because they are too afraid to take risks. They are so afraid to make mistakes and stain their purity or look inadequate in some way. This fear holds them back from following their heart.

Mistakes are a natural part of growth. Without forgiveness of mistakes, we don't feel safe to risk the possibility of making a mistake. Most people are afraid that if they make mistakes, they will lose either love or success forever. The truth is they may incur a loss, but it will not be forever. When you give yourself permission to experiment more and make some mistakes, you open the door for miraculous and accelerated change.

Rigidly holding on to what has worked for others or even for yourself, when your soul wants to experiment and try something different, blocks the river of life energy that wants to flow through you. Often, the fatigue we feel as we get older is the result of blocking our natural life force.

The Outdated Notion of Karma

The old outdated notion of karma is that what you did in your past comes back to you and keeps coming back. For example, what you did in a past life determines the good fortune you have in this life. If you were good, then you get good back in return. Your past creates your future. This same idea is understood in science. For every action there is an equal and opposite reaction. So, if I throw the ball at a wall, it comes back to me. If I send you love, it will come back to me. This now has become common sense, and we are ready for the next level of understanding; your past creates now and right now creates your future.

By learning to use your inner creative power, you can live in the moment and begin consciously creating the future you want. Forgiveness releases you from the influence of the past and frees you to be in the present to create something new. As long as you hold others to the past and resist forgiveness, then you hold yourself in the past and are unable to create a new life from this moment.

If someone stole your money, by forgiving him or her you are free to create even more money from the present time. If, on the other hand, you hold on to your hurt and close your heart, then you perpetuate the loss. Feeling like a victim, you continue to attract or be attracted to situations that make you feel like a victim.

The limitation of the karma theory is that for the rest of your life you must endure the consequences of your past. This is like saying you were born into a poor and uneducated family, and to be happy you must accept your lot in life. Although we would now consider this thought to be absurd, that was the accepted notion in the world for thousands of years.

The principles of democracy on which America was founded are actually incredibly advanced spiritual concepts.

The old concept of karma means your future is determined by what you have done or not done, thought or not thought, believed or not believed, felt or not felt, said or not said, promised or not promised, needed or not needed, etc. The new concept of instant karma is that your future is determined by what you do, think, and feel *today*, and those are now your choice. When people were unaware of their inner world and feelings, they didn't have a choice, but now we are aware or can quickly learn to become aware. By following the nine principles, you are exercising your power to be in the moment and choose your responses to life rather than continuing to react automatically.

In the past, if you got sick and, after going to a healer you weren't healed, then you would conclude you were being punished by God or had to suffer more before you could be redeemed or healed. Jesus, the great teacher and healer, came to dispel this misunderstanding. His message was that everyone is forgiven. The God he spoke of and directly experienced was not punishing in any way, but forgiving. By opening their hearts to Jesus, people were healed regardless of their past.

Karma and Grace

Two thousand years ago, the grace or freedom from past karma that comes with forgiveness was incomprehensible. Although Jesus and other great teachers taught this message to the masses, most people could not understand it. This was a really new idea. Modern teachers deliver this same message of forgiveness, and finally people are getting it. The words are practically the same, but because the shift in world consciousness has occurred, we can get it. We are now ready to open our hearts and experience the grace that comes when we can love again and again as if for the first time.

In the past, people were closed to their true selves and unaware of authentic feelings. They were not conscious of their inner motives, beliefs, and feelings that eventually would determine their words, actions, and results. Without an awareness of their inner world, they were unable to create change. The more aware they are of how they feel, the more they begin to notice that the choices they make interacting in the world generate a mirrorlike reflection.

This does not mean that we are completely responsible for how others behave or for what happens around us, but we do make choices all the time that influence others. Though we are never responsible for others, we do have the power to pull the best or the worst out of a situation. When we are acting from anger and judgment, for example, we will tend to pull anger and judgment from another. When we can release our tendency to close our minds and hearts, then we find more and more that the people with whom we choose to interact are more open to us.

Every parent has experienced that a child, whom you love with all your heart, has the power to evoke from you more interest, compassion, and love. In this way, who we are inside has an influence on the world around us, regardless of what we say or do.

In addition, we affect the world by thoughts, feelings, and desires of which we are not even aware. The good thing about being aware of our deeper inner feelings is that we have the choice to change them and increase our power to extract the best in every situation. Here are some examples:

- Connecting with your true peaceful self doesn't make a shopping line go faster, but it awakens your intuition to pick a faster line.

- Connecting with your joyful self doesn't bring a loved one back to life, but it does help you heal your grief and remember the happy times you had together. It motivates you to move on and rebuild your life and find love, joy, and happiness again.

- Connecting with your confident self doesn't give you all the answers or cause others to trust you, but it does motivate you to see your mistakes more clearly. It motivates you to seek out useful help when needed so that you make fewer mistakes and can earn the trust of others.

- Connecting with your loving self doesn't ensure that your partner will always be loving toward you, but it does affect the way you say things and react to what your partner says. In this manner, you do have the power to inspire the best that he or she has to give at that time.

The magic of miracles is simply to remove the blocks that prevent us from distilling the best each situation has to offer and then move forward. This concept becomes an experience as you become more aware of what you are projecting.

Some people struggle to have a positive mood but then wonder why people are so nasty to them. There are many reasons for this. Instant karma is not the only principle that governs our relationship with the outer world.

It could be people are mean to you because you are not following your soul desire, and the world is resisting you. Simply, you are swimming upstream, so naturally life is more difficult. It could also be that you are drawn to mean people in your life to teach you understanding and tolerance. Often, when our souls want to grow, we are attracted to situations that will challenge us and make us stronger. There are a variety of factors that determine our outer world and some over which we have no control.

To understand karma and our personal responsibility in life, it is important that we do not conclude that everything is the result of past karma. It is time to update our thinking with open minds and hearts that can consider many ideas and possibilities at once. It is important to recognize in this age of miracles that any belief that prevents you from feeling good about yourself and does not inspire you is either incorrect or just misunderstood. This is a time of great housecleaning for the world. It is a time to clean out the things that really do not serve us and to create more room for new ideas and beliefs that can serve our new potential to create miracles.

7

OUR NINE
PRIMARY NEEDS

There are nine primary needs that, when met, give us the power to create practical miracles. Though each is always required, depending upon our age, one particular need becomes especially important or significant as we continue to develop and mature through life.

At each stage of life, about every seven years, a significant change occurs and a new need emerges. For the next seven years, this new need becomes our most important motivator. By fulfilling it, we are able to develop our age-appropriate potential and provide the basis for optimum improvement in the next stage.

Without the appropriate support we require at each stage, we are unable to realize our full inner potential. At a later stage, we struggle even harder because we have not been adequately prepared or supported previously. In this way, to some degree we are held back by our past.

Without the support we require, we are unable to realize our inner potential.

This limitation can be overcome. As adults becoming aware of what we haven't gotten, we can take responsibility for filling the void and giving to ourselves what we didn't get before.

For example, if a child doesn't get enough sleep or food, his body will not develop in the radiant, healthy manner to which it is designed. We grown-ups are no longer dependent on our parents to give us what we need. We can give ourselves plentiful sleep and the healthy food we missed, and at last create the basis for vibrant health.

Likewise, not getting enough love and support to feel good about ourselves will affect and limit all later stages of development. Many of our limitations and struggles in the present come from the unfulfilled needs in our past. By taking some time to recognize what we didn't get, we can realize more clearly what we need to give to ourselves in present time.

Fortunately, we now have the power to give ourselves the love and support we missed and overcome the limitations of our past. As we explore the ideal conditions of development, keep in mind that they are *ideal* and that no one ever gets it all. We all grow up in a limited and challenging world, but, ultimately, as we learn to meet those challenges, in spite of how we may have been deprived, we can grow stronger.

By recognizing what you missed you can awaken the suppressed or denied parts of your true self. Through this process new opportunities open up for you to experience incredible growth and transformation. By beginning to give yourself what you missed, you will experience the power of creating practical miracles. Let's take a look at the nine different age periods and the primary needs for each stage of development.

Stage 1: Vulnerability, Nurturing, and Dependence

From birth to age seven, we primarily follow our parents' leadership. Our primary way of learning is through imitating them. If they love us, then we learn to regard ourselves as worthy of love and support. If they are responsible, then we gradually learn to trust.

When we are given plenty of love in our first seven years, we are then able to be vulnerable and develop our ability to recognize our needs. The more we trust that we can get what we need, the more aware we are of our needs. A neglected child is most often unaware of his or her real needs.

With a history of getting the support we need, as we grow older we automatically assume that things will go our way. Generally speaking, addictive cravings, mistrust, or neediness develop when we are deprived of such early basic needs as loving kindness and attention, understanding, security, food, sleep, routine, and affection.

When our cries are heard and nurtured in infancy and childhood, we experience healthy hope and optimism. We are quickly inspired to grow, change, and improve our lives. We have a solid foundation for nurturing ourselves and others later in life. If someone was there for you as a youngster in a time of need, then later in life it is easier to ask for help as well as be there for others. This stage is the basis for the first principle of creating practical miracles: **Believe as if miracles are possible.**

Stage 2: Fun, Friendship, and Interdependence

From age seven to fourteen, we primarily follow the rules. Playing structured games and following specific rules ensures us the safety to explore being ourselves. Play teaches us to enjoy the process for itself rather than making our happiness dependent on winning or being the best. We learn through experience that friendship, sharing, and cooperation create the greatest fulfillment.

With the support and security of friendship, in our next seven years we are able to develop our ability to enjoy life, have fun, and be happy. With enough support to have fun, we are able to learn that "it's just a game" and that having fun is more important than winning. With enough fun, we learn that our greatest happiness comes not from whether we win or lose, but from how we play the game.

In this stage, a child learns that winning is certainly fun, but how we play is more fulfilling.

As we experience that we don't have to win in order to be loved, we develop our ability to have fun regardless of the result. Team games are also especially good, because even though we may not have the skills to win, our team may win, and we are part of the team. If our team loses, we know that defeat is not due to "our bad luck," incompetence, or inadequacy. With playful support, we become uninhibited and can more fully express ourselves. We are able to appreciate the support we get from others and, in return, courageously take risks to give support.

In this stage, with the safety net of our parents' unconditional love, we begin daring to express who we are without worrying about what others think about us. Lacking pressure to behave, look good, or perform in a certain way, we gradually master cause and effect; we learn that giving is almost always reciprocated. This inner security provides the basis for the second principle of creating practical miracles: **Live as if you are free to do what you want.**

Without a pressure to be a certain way or to perform, we gradually master cause and effect.

Sharing and cooperation are easily developed when we are not pressured by responsibilities. Too much emphasis today is placed on household chores. Rather than raising children who could have fun helping their parents do tasks, parents mistakenly make children solely responsible for specific duties to be done alone. In addition, we send our kids to schools that are often anything but fun and where too much homework is given.

Education during this age can be challenging, but ideally it must be fun. When this stage is not filled with games, playing, group activities, and enjoyment, it's often difficult to have fun or to be happy later in life. If we receive the fun and friendship needed at this stage, then as teenagers and for the rest of our lives we will be prepared to settle down and work hard to meet life's increasing demands. Through meeting this need, we develop the ability to enjoy hard work.

Stage 3: Achievement, Self-reliance, and Independence

From age fourteen to twenty-one, we primarily follow what we consider to be reasonable. We are still dependent on others for guidance, but we are primarily dependent on doing what is reasonable to us. The quality of our growth is directly proportional to the reasonableness or fairness of our parents, teachers, leaders, role models, and peers. Without proper or reasonable adult supervision and inspiring leadership, teens become swayed by misguided peer pressure, which is often detrimental to growth.

In our teenage years, with sufficient motivation and opportunities to test ourselves, we are able to develop confidence in our ability to achieve. In this stage, we rely more on ourselves and patiently pursue our goals without expecting perfection. We are more relaxed and peaceful because we are capable of trusting others and being receptive to their support.

We are thus able to forgive easily and self-correct when we make mistakes. We are clearly beginners and therefore are open and receptive to feedback from those older than us. We are open to help, while also learning to do things independently. Our competence and confidence grows in spurts as we continue to glimpse our newfound ability to rely on ourselves. When setbacks are expected and high achievement is not demanded, teens can assert their increasing need for independence without rebelling.

This stage is the time for testing ourselves. We are not yet on our own, so we don't feel an unhealthy pressure to be perfect. We learn freely from mistakes and do our best to achieve. With the right teachers and role models, we have an example of what we want to be while retaining the freedom to learn gradually. This stage provides the basis for the third principle of creating miracles: **Learn as if you are a beginner.**

Stage 4: Love, Experience, and Self-sufficiency

From age twenty-one to twenty-eight, we primarily follow our hearts. In this stage we need to do what we love while growing and learning through new experiences. Leaving home and gradually separating from dependence on our parents allow us to develop a healthy sense of self-sufficiency. During this stage, it is important for our parents to relinquish control but still be there if we need their support. Ideally, during this period, parents and role models still serve as a safety net, which frees us to take risks and explore life.

Our increased autonomy gives us the opportunity to grow in love for others and ourselves without expectations or demands. We can take life lightly because we haven't yet assumed the responsibilities of a long-term, committed relationship. We can effortlessly let go of our hurts because we are less dependent on others for their love and support. Even if we do get seriously involved, we can maintain a healthy distance that allows both people to continue to develop as individuals.

We can effortlessly let go of our hurts when we are less dependent on others for their love and support.

The secret of growth in this stage is to give up dependence on others and discover our own self-sufficiency. In the past, without equal opportunities to support themselves, most women who are now over thirty-five were deprived of this experience. Lack of freedom caused them to be overly dependent on men or on what men can provide. Fortunately, women today can compensate for this loss. This shift frees a woman from expecting or requiring too much from her intimate partner in terms of love and support.

People who do not follow their hearts are often too critical of themselves or others. This new freedom to explore who we are and what we can achieve increases our self-esteem. By doing what we want, not what others will have us to do, we begin to accept, appreciate, and admire ourselves. Along with this healthy self-esteem, we develop a sense of gratitude.

When we feel good about ourselves, without overdepending on others, we are truly free to acknowledge the many blessings in our life as well as its wealth of new and exciting possibilities. This stage provides the basis for the fourth principle of creating miracles: **Love as if for the first time.**

Stage 5: Intimacy, Communication, and Generosity

From age twenty-eight to thirty-five, we primarily follow our conscience. We learn to do what we believe to be right, regardless of what someone else says or does. When we can get to know someone else intimately and, having seen the best and worst of him or her, we can still love that person, then real and lasting love is realized. Embracing this higher truth, we are able to give love freely, regardless of what our partner gives to us.

Instead of giving according to what we could get or have already gotten, we choose how much to give according to the dictates of our conscience. In simpler terms, just because someone hurts you doesn't justify hurting that person back. Even being rejected in a relationship doesn't justify withholding the love you had intended to give. Though this notion should be taught to children, it is not until this stage that we can fully put it into practice.

Our spirit can soar because others do not limit us in determining our willingness to give of ourselves. We are always free to give. For example, if I want to be generous, and someone makes a mistake and offends me, I can still choose to be generous. I don't have to lower myself to get even, punish, or teach a lesson.

Giving support at this stage becomes a personal choice, often inspired by successful communication. Previously we learned to be open to everyone and every possibility, but now we can give more of ourselves to one person and less of ourselves to another. The secret here is giving from choice, not according to how someone else has treated us. This is the basis of intimacy—we make one person more special than others.

If I have a million dollars to distribute and I give it to a million people, then every person gets one dollar. This kind of giving is not as deeply meaningful or satisfying to me or to them. But if I take my million dollars and give it to one person, the gift is mutually much more fulfilling and supportive.

Being in an intimate relationship is like giving your million dollars to one person rather than a million. An exclusively monogamous, intimate relationship offers the opportunity for couples to experience the highest degree of giving their love and support. It is this giving more that helps us to realize how much more we have to give.

An exclusively monogamous, intimate relationship offers the opportunity for couples to experience the highest degree of giving.

Having already developed a healthy sense of self-reliance and self-sufficiency, we can love and nurture ourselves without depending so much on our partner. Only then are we truly free to give love unconditionally. Instead of needing our partner's love and support, our primary need in this stage is to give love. As love grows, we are able to give more freely in all areas without limiting ourselves or holding back when circumstances are not ideal.

Instead of needing our intimate partner's love and support, our primary need is to give love.

With the experience of greater intimacy that evolves in a mature, committed relationship, we can continue to develop our ability to connect and relate to others. With greater self-awareness of our limitations as well as those of our partner, we grow in humility and acceptance.

This new openness gives us the compassion to respect our partner's differences and create together something greater than we could create alone. By increasing our ability to listen, communicate, and share, we become more influential and powerful in all areas of our life. This stage provides the basis for the fifth principle of creating miracles: **Give as if you already have what you need.**

Stage 6: Responsibility, Accountability, and Commitment

From age thirty-five to forty-two, we primarily follow our sense of duty. It is the time to take responsibility for more than yourself and your intimate partner. You make promises and commitments and do your best to honor your word and your values. In this way, we begin to grow into greater love and to make a difference in the world.

With the experience of parenthood or the increased duties we have assumed by our midthirties, we awaken to a greater sense of commitment and integrity. Possessing a healthy sense of self, we are able to regulate how much we give to others through choice, not obligation. At this point, we can assume responsibility for others without losing ourselves or promising more than we can deliver.

Being more responsible for others leads us to the increased wisdom and inner guidance that allows us to be more accountable for correcting our mistakes and becoming more creative. As we do this without sacrificing ourselves, we find we have more to give. This is when we can begin having a much greater impact in the world. Our personal potential is not only realized, but it also has a chance to grow and become more powerful. In this stage, we can begin to make our mark in the world.

As we take on more responsibilities without sacrificing ourselves, we have more to give.

With increasing accountability, we are able to recognize how we contribute to the success or failure of every situation and circumstance that we confront. We are able to appreciate our strengths while also recognizing our weaknesses and limitations. This new degree of accountability allows us the wisdom to acknowledge that every life experience is and always has been an opportunity to grow and to learn.

Increased accountability provides as well a sense of authorship in our lives. With new confidence, we gain access to more energy and the strength to persist in meeting life's challenges.

In this stage, we make choices primarily from our need to care for others and fulfill our duties, rather than just the personal satisfaction that comes from giving love and support. While struggling to balance my commitments to work, my marriage, and my children, I was able to draw on much more energy and power. I trusted that by caring for my family first, my success—although not immediate—would eventually flourish and last.

As success increased, my greatest challenge was to not be tempted by all the opportunities that success brought and to keep my priorities in order. I was able to sustain this by never making work more important than my family.

Without good communication with my wife regarding her wishes and the needs of our children, I would never have accomplished what I have. By staying balanced, I found my personal power and success could gradually build. In addition, living simply within my financial means made it much easier to make my family, not money, my first priority. This stage provides the basis for the sixth principle of creating miracles: **Work as if money doesn't matter.**

Stage 7: Service, Contribution, and Creativity

From age forty-two to forty-nine, we primarily follow our dreams. Maturity dawns in our forties. When we are young, we learn to be independent and self-sufficient. We test our wings and focus on discovering and developing our inner potential. In our thirties, we begin to use and expand that potential to give freely of ourselves without depending on others. As a result, we become more adept at recognizing and expressing our inner creative power. This experience heralds the dawn of increased selflessness and a willingness to serve others.

Deep inside, everyone has a unique dream for making a difference in the world. It may be to write a book, start a healing center, invent a cure, help the homeless, run for public office, join a cause, be the first to climb a mountain, or some other aspiration. This dream may be to help others directly or it may be to inspire or even entertain them. The more we are able to put ourselves aside, the more creative we can be. This creativity becomes the basis for making our dreams come true.

**Deep inside, everyone has a unique dream
for making a difference in the world.**

In each example, a big part of our dream is to positively influence our community and our world. In this seventh stage, our fulfillment comes mainly from serving others and making a contribution. Our personal reward is increased creativity, as our creative power is enhanced when we take time to consider quietly our deep-seated desire to make a difference. Though this principle is true at every stage of development, it is particularly significant in our forties for our personal fulfillment and development.

Keeping our commitments and thereby mining more personal power provides the basis for increasing creativity. As serving others becomes our primary motive, our attachment to the results of our own actions is minimized. We are freed from the tendency to repeat what has worked in the past and can create anew in each moment.

Creativity is not just painting a picture or composing a song. It is the much more expansive ability to approach every situation with fresh insight and with a new approach when one is needed. We flow through life making the necessary adjustments for solving problems and improving the world. The increased expression of creativity provides the basis for the seventh principle for creating practical miracles: **Relax as if everything will be okay.**

Stage 8: Spirituality, Healing, and Balance

From age forty-nine to fifty-six we primarily follow our higher power or God. In our younger years, we asked God to help us, but in this stage of life, we have finally grown up and now ask to serve God. We can certainly do it at an earlier stage, but at this time, asking to serve becomes our foremost need. The active surrender of our ego to the will of God creates maximum fulfillment.

This does not entail having to sacrifice our other needs. It simply means that for us to be most completely fulfilled, our main focus should be serving God or the divine plan. This is done through nurturing others as well as ourselves. Our challenge in this stage is to find this healthy and healing balance.

One basic way to recognize the divine plan is realizing that every activity and experience in your life occurred to teach you an important lesson. As we find the reward in every challenge and heal every wound to become stronger, then we can, with greater awareness, participate in God's plan for us.

At this stage, we grow more adept at interpreting situations in the moment as gifts and teachings. Challenges become opportunities to serve God, not merely to serve ourselves. Our experience of God as a tangible but invisible reality becomes more vivid and fulfilling.

**Challenging situations become opportunities
to serve God, not merely to serve ourselves.**

One of the reasons small children enjoy the game of peek-a-boo is that their brains have not yet fully developed. They are literally unable to comprehend that, although you are not visible, you are still present. To a child, when you move behind a screen, you have actually vanished. When you reappear to them, it is as if you have suddenly returned from nowhere. This mysterious occurrence makes children laugh and provides them with lots of fun.

Gradually, as the brain continues to develop, a child can comprehend that even though you are not visibly present, you are still available and they are not alone. When you momentarily move behind the screen, they realize that you are still there but not visible to their senses. At this point in brain development, even if the child is playing in one room, he or she feels comforted knowing that Mom or Dad, although not actually in the room, is available somewhere else in the house.

This example resembles our spiritual growth. We are all like children when it comes to knowing God. In our younger years, we are unable to comprehend fully that God can exist even if we cannot see God. By witnessing the results of God's magic and miracles, we experience wonder and awe. Eventually, we begin to sense that God is always present, and we can call on God's support whenever we need it.

Today this awareness has become more universal. Everyone at any age can know God more directly by creating practical miracles. Although we cannot see God, we can feel God's presence. We can call on God for help and receive additional support. A lifetime of receiving this support prepares us to know and surrender fully to God in service.

**Everyone at any age can know God more directly
by creating practical miracles.**

Expressing our creative potential in the previous stage prepares us for this vivid experience of God. When we first use our inner power to create, it is easy to assume that we are solely responsible for the creation. However, once our creativity begins to flow freely, we begin to clearly experience that this power comes from some other source. In a sense we "will it" and then it comes through us.

Whether or not we call this source God, we are starting to realize we are not the one really doing the creating. Certainly, we arrived at the creative insight or hunch, but, at the same time, we have no sense of where it came from. One moment we are puzzled, and in the next moment, the answer just appears. Like children playing peek-a-boo, we are amazed.

Once my creativity as a writer started to flow, I was exhilarated, but I was also disconcerted. The day after a great writing session, I felt very insecure. I would read what I had written and think, "I don't know how I did that and so I don't know if I can do it again." Once I relaxed and began to trust that I just needed to calm down and ask for the help, it always came.

When I first began giving successful lectures, I would worry before each talk, because I didn't have a clue as to how I made people laugh. It just happened as soon as I was in front of an audience and the creativity started to flow. I gradually began to trust that my creativity would be there and stopped fretting. This paved the way for my recognition that it is always God who creates through us and with us. In this way, we are always in partnership with God. Although I do it, I also don't do it.

With success comes the increased recognition that it is always God who creates through us and with us.

This paradox can easily be understood from another common experience. When we drive a car, we are driving the car. Yet, from another perspective, the car is driving us and taking us where we want to go. Both concepts are accurate. You start the car, you push the accelerator and brakes, you drive, but it is the engine that gets you going. In a similar manner, we indeed drive the car, but God is the engine that delivers us to our destination.

This evolution of our awareness of God is nurtured from life's previous stages. In our younger years, we have a greater awareness of what we do, but as we mature we become conscious of what God does. This increasing consciousness becomes the basis for creating more practical miracles. When we ignore our access to God's support, our powers are greatly limited. On the other hand, if we expect God to do it all for us, then we also are limited. Practical miracles can occur only when we perform them together with God.

If we just expect God to do it all for us, then we are also limited.

In our thirties, by giving more of ourselves and taking on responsibilities, we grow in personal power. Our success in life generates a need to give back in kind the gifts we have received. By serving others in our forties while also continuing to meet our needs, we are free to experience a much greater increase of personal power, creativity, love, or success. As we give back, we are freed from the limits of our individuality and experience an increased flow of God's generous nature and bounty.

**Our success in life generates a need to give back
what we have received with service.**

Whether or not we believe in God, we naturally become more spiritual. When we increase awareness of our inner spirit then good fortune, grace, and luck increase. We see the wonders of God everywhere and are now highly capable of creating practical miracles.

Life becomes a wonderful, enriching experience of healing others and healing ourselves. This is the time we can get out of the way and really experience the flow of God's grace in our lives. We become clearly aware that we are partners with God in service to others as well as to ourselves. The increased spirituality, healing, and balance in this stage provide the basis for the eighth principle for creating practical miracles: **Talk to God as if you are being heard.**

Stage 9: Being, Fulfillment, and Growth

From age fifty-six and onward we primarily follow our destiny. In this stage we discover that there really is nowhere we have to go or no particular way we have be. Just being ourselves is enough. To the extent that we have nurtured ourselves during the other eight stages, this is a time of great fulfillment. Our fulfillment primarily comes from just being ourselves and discovering in each moment the new aspect of being that keeps coming out of ourselves in every situation.

We realize that everything we need is always present and that all we need to do in order to serve God, the world, and ourselves is simply to be ourselves. Automatically our purpose in life unfolds and is fulfilled. By simply being ourselves we are able to fulfill our destiny.

In this stage we are free of all personal needs to change circumstances or get anywhere. We can be fulfilled with whatever comes our way because it pulls out more of who we are. When this is our daily experience, we concretely experience that every moment brings out a new part of who we are.

Every moment is either the fulfillment of a desire or a challenge to help draw out and strengthen our soul.

In this stage, there is no specific agenda because life is a big and wonderful mystery that continues to surprise us with wonder. We may still have agendas, but we are always free to adjust them. Our main agenda is to simply be ourselves and discover what the next moment will pull out of us to serve the greater good, which also includes us.

In this way, we continue to grow. It is like paddling in a boat and then relaxing for a moment to discover that the river will take you where you are going. You don't know where that is, but you trust that it will just continue to nourish and support you as it always has.

You delightfully realize that the river was always carrying you and leading you on to greater growth, even when in the past you thought you had to do it. In this stage you realize that nothing is certain because life is always changing. At the same time, you experience that everything that happens can and does support you in some way.

Just being yourself doesn't mean that you passively sit around all day and do nothing. You continue on as you have—wanting, needing, intending, wishing, choosing, liking, thinking, and feeling. The big difference is that all the time your main fulfillment comes primarily from being true to yourself regardless of the circumstances. What you are motivated to do or not do is all in God's hands.

In this stage you feel a greater freedom to be yourself at all times. Your greatest fulfillment comes by simply being true to yourself in every reaction and response to life. The incredible fulfillment that is possible in this stage comes with the realization that every moment provides an opportunity for us to express our highest self.

Although it sounds like it is some kind of perfect state, it is not. Life may bring cold weather, but then we are grateful for the warmth within ourselves that comes up in response. Others may reject us or scorn us, but then we find our fulfillment through experiencing the love and forgiveness that emerges from our heart.

Life is still filled with both gain and loss, pleasure and pain, but in this stage our fulfillment comes from feeling the appropriate response in our heart. For example, when we experience the pain of loss, then also we feel a wave of appreciation swelling in our hearts for what we lost. When we experience gain, we feel a wave of appreciation for what we do have. In this way, circumstances no longer hold the importance they had before.

Every situation becomes an opportunity to pull forth greater peace, joy, confidence, love, patience, optimism, strength, humility, fulfillment, inspiration, courage, and innocence. These twelve primary attributes of our true self have an opportunity to emerge in every situation, good or bad, difficult or easy, positive or negative.

Most people in this stage are unable to experience this fulfillment because they have not yet learned who they are or how to access their true self at challenging times. When, however, these skills have been developed, then every bump on the road brings us fulfillment because it gives us an opportunity to simply be ourselves and enjoy the ride.

Every situation presents us with the wonderful new experience of being ourselves in a different way. Life becomes a huge feast with unlimited possibilities for fulfillment because all we really want is the opportunity to be ourselves once again in each moment. It is this realization in the ninth stage that provides the foundation for fully living the ninth principle: **Feast as if you can have whatever you want.**

Few people in previous generations have been prepared to appreciate this stage. Having spent their previous years unable to fulfill past needs or do the required healing to fill in the holes, they experience at this stage different degrees of sickness, regret, and fatigue. Now, through learning to correct this situation and nurture their different needs, instead of preparing to die, they can look forward to unlimited growth.

With the power to create practical miracles, anyone can access this power to heal their past and live out his or her life with lasting love, increasing success, and vibrant health. At any stage, regardless of one's past, one can begin accessing the powers appropriate to his or her age and begin creating practical miracles. Even when sick and on their way to die, people can awaken their body's healing power so that the dying process is easier and more peaceful for them.

For easy reference, these nine needs and stages of development can be summarized in the following manner:

The Nine Needs and Stages of Development

Stage 1: Birth to seven. Follow the leader.
   Need: Vulnerability, Nurturing, and Dependence

Stage 2: Seven to fourteen. Follow the rules.
   Need: Fun, Friendship, and Interdependence

Stage 3: Fourteen to twenty-one. Follow your reason.
   Need: Achievement, Self-reliance, and Independence

Stage 4: Twenty-one to twenty-eight. Follow your heart.
   Need: Love, Experience, and Self-sufficiency

Stage 5: Twenty-eight to thirty-five. Follow your conscience.
   Need: Intimacy, Communication, and Generosity

Stage 6: Thirty-five to forty-two. Follow your duty.
   Need: Responsibility, Accountability, and Commitment

Stage 7: Forty-two to forty-nine. Follow your dreams.
   Need: Service, Contribution, and Creativity

Stage 8: Forty-nine to fifty-six. Follow your higher power or God.
   Need: Spirituality, Healing, and Balance

Stage 9: Fifty-six and beyond. Follow your destiny.
   Need: Being, Fulfillment, and Growth

8
—
THE BALANCING ACT
OF LIFE

Balancing our different needs is required throughout our lives. Even when one need is uppermost, we must still continue to support, to varying degrees, all of our others. This process becomes easier to perform when we know what to look for and give ourselves permission to have different needs.

Nurturing our unfolding needs can be easily visualized by imagining yourself as a performer who spins and balances nine plates on nine poles. You begin by spinning the first plate on the first pole. As long as the plate spins, it stays balanced. If it is not kept spinning, then it will begin to wobble and soon fall off the pole. Once a plate is spinning, less time is required to maintain its balance.

After spinning the first plate, you then spin the next. Before proceeding to spin the third plate, you must briefly respin the first plate to keep it going and balanced. Then you are ready to move on to the third plate. After spinning it, you must quickly go back and respin the first and second plates to keep them spinning.

You can then proceed to the fourth plate. In this way, you eventually have all nine plates spinning. To sustain this balancing feat, however, you have to keep moving back and forth among the plates. As one plate begins to wobble, you give it a little spin. Then another begins to teeter and you correct it. By your attending to the different plates in this way, they all stay balanced and the crowd begins to cheer.

This balancing act is the challenge we all face in life. Keeping all the plates in your life spinning provides you with the basic process for creating practical miracles at work, in your relationships, and in your health. Though everyone has the same nine plates, we must also remember that each person is unique and has plates of different sizes.

One person may require additional love and intimacy, while another may need more work and fun. A third person may hunger for greater spirituality. The combinations and possibilities are endless. For everyone to experience success and fulfillment in life, there is never just one answer or solution. The awareness of our different needs presents a broad map to help us discover what is best for ourselves.

Looking for Support in All the Wrong Places

Understanding the nature of our true needs is not always so straightforward and obvious. Most people have had the experience of wanting, needing, craving, or longing to have something, and then, when they got it, found it was insufficient or made them sick. We often think we know what is good for us, but then find that we are not satisfied.

For example, food is a valid need, but if we are not meeting our other needs, we may begin to depend on food to satisfy us more than we really need it. Unless we are also meeting our other needs, then we may become addicted to food and feel a compulsion to overeat.

Quite often we suffer in life because we are tending to one need and not to our other needs. We may be spinning one plate but suffering because all the others keep falling down. Yet, unless we are aware of the other plates, we will keep spinning just one, hoping that one day it will be as fulfilling as it used to be.

Without an awareness of what we really need and access to that support, it is very difficult to stop an unhealthy craving. This same difficult task becomes miraculously easy when we can first clearly realize in our minds that what we want is not good for us, and then clearly know what it is that we really need.

There are four obvious signs that we are looking in the wrong direction for what we need. A greater awareness of these indicators will assist us in recognizing them so that we can quickly shift our focus to our other needs. If these signs appear, one or more of our plates is wobbling and requires us to shift our attention to them.

Use these indicators to realize that you need to shift your focus of attention to what you really need. Instead of continuing to spin one plate, move to another. The four signs are:

1. We are mentally stressed, feeling upset, empty, pressured, bored, annoyed, desperate, overwhelmed, restless, irritated, offended, nervous, or tense.

2. We are emotionally distressed, feeling anger, sadness, fear, sorrow, frustration, disappointment, worry, embarrassment, rage, hurt, panic, and shame.

3. We are blocked from feeling peace, joy, confidence, love, patience, optimism, strength, humility, fulfillment, inspiration, courage, and innocence. These qualities of our true self are often being blocked when we experience resent-

ment, depression, confusion, indifference, judgment, procrastination, indecision, perfectionism, jealousy, self-pity, anxiety, and guilt.

4. Whenever we are sick, we experience chronic pain, physical weakness, or chronic fatigue.

Within each of these levels, there are four additional signs that indicate we are looking in the wrong place for satisfaction:

1. Whenever we demand more than we can easily get, we are usually overlooking our other needs.

2. Whenever we remember all the times we didn't get what we needed to justify our wanting more, then what we are demanding is not our correct need. It is usually unrealistic, and ultimately it will not create lasting fulfillment.

3. Whenever we pine for the past, when we got more, or compare what we have now to what we had then, and "now" comes up short, then we are missing the mark.

4. Whenever we accept what we have but don't truly appreciate what we are getting, then we are ignoring our true needs.

Different Needs for Different People

We must always keep in mind that different people possess different degrees of each of the nine needs. One person may have a substantial need for intimacy and unconditional loving, but a smaller need for work and achievement. Still another may have a greater need for spirituality and a lesser one for intimacy. In this way, every person has different degrees of each need. By nurturing one more intensely and another less, they will be most fulfilled.

Although simple, this concept is easy to misunderstand. People who consistently have problems fulfilling a particular need or feel powerless to achieve what they need are usually looking in the wrong direction for support. They mistakenly believe that more of one need will make them happier, when what they really need is something else. Here are some examples of this behavior:

Nine Illusions of Life

If nurturing makes you happy, then more nurturing will make you happier.

If play makes you happy, then more play will make you happier.

If achievement makes you happy, then more achievement will make you happier.

If self-sufficiency makes you happy, then more self-sufficiency will make you happier.

If intimacy makes you happy, then more intimacy will make you happier.

If responsibility makes you happy, then more responsibility will make you happier.

If service makes you happy, then more service will make you happier.

If spiritual growth makes you happy, then more spiritual growth will make you happier.

If being you makes you happy, then just being you will make you even happier.

The promise that "more is better" is a grand illusion. Seeking more of what you don't need more of is the root

cause of all unhappiness. If you are seeking what you genuinely need, you are happy in the process and have moved
beyond "more is better."

The promise that "more is better" is a big illusion.

When a car is low on oil, the radiator is steaming, or a
tire is flat, it should not be driven until repairs and correc-
tions are made. Likewise, we should, if possible, seek to
understand and heal stressed and distressed reactions before
deciding how we should respond. Making decisions when
you are hurt, angry, or scared just doesn't work. We cannot
create cooperation to get what we need when we are stressed
and distressed. When we are equipped to see through the
illusions of life in this way, then we can create a fulfilled and
creative existence by balancing all our needs.

The Need for Healing

It is customary to go through a healing crisis at the beginning of each of the nine stages. This time is generally a window of opportunity to feel and heal past deficiencies. Quite
often, people will experience various challenges and sometimes their greatest challenges come during the year after
these birthdays: six, thirteen, twenty, twenty-seven, thirty-
four, forty-one, forty-eight, and fifty-five. The year after
your sixth birthday is actually the beginning of your seventh
year. The year after your thirteenth birthday is the beginning
of your fourteenth year, and so on.

To the degree that people ignore their needs for healing at
these junction points, they are somewhat held back from
being fully successful in the next stage. Then, in the next
stage their bodies may begin to get sick, their relationships
may become disappointing, or their business may go downhill.

In order for us to heal, we can awaken our body's healing potential by getting the support we couldn't or didn't receive when we were younger. Because our wounds are different, healing is always different for every one. Depending on our different deficiencies in life, these are some examples of activities that could be most fulfilling and healing. Stage by stage, these are some examples of what a person may choose to heal:

If you didn't experience enough love and nurturing in Stage 1 (birth to seven years), you may feel a need for therapy to heal.

If you didn't experience enough fun in Stage 2 (age seven to fourteen), you may need to have more fun and enjoy your life and the fruits of your labors.

If you didn't work and experience greater achievement in your teens during Stage 3 (age fourteen to twenty-one), you may buckle down and work harder than ever before or go back to school.

If you didn't experience enough autonomy in Stage 4 (age twenty-one to twenty-eight), you may suddenly seek to do the things you never could do before or travel to places you always wanted to visit.

If you didn't experience real intimacy in Stage 5 (age twenty-eight to thirty-five), you may hunger for a healing romance or a torrid affair.

If you didn't have children or increased responsibility in Stage 6 (age thirty-five to forty-two), you may want to start a family, care for a pet, grow a garden, or even start a new business. You may suddenly find yourself interested in politics or joining a group devoted to a noble cause.

If you didn't follow your dreams in Stage 7 (age forty-two to forty-nine), or express yourself in some creative way, you may take up painting, writing, singing, acting, or playing a musical instrument in order to heal. Or, you may accept a new, creative, and challenging project to serve your community, help the poor, or clean up the environment.

If you didn't develop your spirituality in Stage 8 (age forty-nine to fifty-six), or even rejected spirituality, you may experience a renewed interest in your spiritual roots or find some other way of giving meaning to your life.

If you didn't let yourself just "be" in Stage 9 (age fifty-six and beyond), you may feel the need to relax and trust the flow of life. You may wish to let go and just be yourself without any worries.

Healing the Past Without Losing What We Have Gained

Particularly in Stage 8, our challenge while healing the past is to fulfill our emerging needs without rejecting the support we have managed to secure in our lives. Although these sudden needs and urges appear to become our primary ones, they are, in fact, temporary. The true consistent need is for healing. As we focus on meeting a past need, we must be careful at the same time to nurture our other ones. These are some examples:

Stage 1. *"To follow our leader"* in order to get nurturing and support, make sure that you don't give away your power and cause even more problems. Often, when you have suppressed yourself to accommodate or please others, at some point later in life these old urges will recur. When they do, they are often distorted and give you an inaccurate reflection of who you truly are, as well as others. You must remember that this recurrence comes from the childlike part of you.

As children, we should follow our leaders, but we require supportive parents in the process. When we throw a tantrum or cry for milk, our mother feeds us. If as adults we cry for milk, we must remember that we are not children and cannot expect others to feed us. It is inappropriate to throw tantrums or demand more just because you are not getting the treatment or support you feel you deserve. Although our feelings are a source of enormous power, they can easily mislead us when our minds and hearts are not also open.

During the healing process, you may find all kinds of intense emotions and reactions returning with a vengeance. A wise person takes responsibility first for healing these reactions, then later makes decisions to create change.

We have no right to expect our intimate partner, children, or work associates to fulfill our unmet needs. If we are unable to heal on our own, then it is time to hire a therapist who can help. In therapy, we can take time each week to receive the vital support we didn't get as a child. Gradually, we will learn to give support and be able to wean ourselves from treatment.

Stage 2. *"To follow the rules"* in the pursuit of finding lasting happiness and joy, don't fall into the trap of feeling guilty. If you have abused yourself or others, recognize your guilt, but forgive yourself and realize that you were doing the best you could. Don't use this new awareness of your mistakes and a willingness to make amends to justify punishing yourself. Acknowledge and learn from your mistakes, then make amends whenever appropriately possible. You can learn from your mistakes only if you can also forgive yourself.

Be careful not to become judgmental when others don't do what you think is right. A sign of genuine self-forgiveness is the ability to forgive and understand others who have made similar mistakes.

In addition, if your mistake was in working too hard, don't give up all work in order to have fun. Gradually work less and gradually have more fun. To correct the mistakes of the past, avoid making another mistake by rejecting work altogether. We can work less or we can change careers, but we don't have to give up work and achievement altogether.

Stage 3. *"To follow reason"* in the pursuit of learning and developing some new skill, we must make sure we don't surrender our own sense of logic. Just because someone has expertise or has developed a skill we lack doesn't make that person better suited to know what is right for us. We must be careful in our willingness to learn from the experts. We must at the same time rely on ourselves to know and determine what we need. When we don't know what this is, it is fine to follow as long as we consider it an experiment. Then, using our own logic and reason, we must go on to determine what we believe to be true. This is a good time to pursue learning a new perspective.

Stage 4. *"To follow our hearts"* and in the pursuit of new experiences to realize greater self-sufficiency, we should not disregard our commitments. When we crave being young again, our partner suddenly looks old or our career seems stale and boring. The answer is not in rejecting our partner or our career for someone younger or something different. The solution is in finding inner happiness by experiencing greater self-sufficiency. Taking some time to do whatever you want to do independently while also respecting your commitments will make you feel young again. This is a good time to take a vacation alone.

Stage 5. *"To follow our conscience"* and give more love through intimacy, we should not end a passionless marriage. Rather than thinking we have to change partners, we can instead change the way we communicate and begin creating more romance in our present relationship. By looking only to change ourselves, we are free from feeling dependent on our partners. We are then liberated to fulfill our longing to give more of our love, and our passion is ignited again. This is a good time to take a relationship workshop or personal growth seminar either together or alone.

Stage 6. *"To follow our integrity"* we should make sure to honor our commitments and to be responsible to ourselves. Sacrifice is never required. When we nurture our needs first, then we have more to give. We must recognize that some promises are not possible or appropriate to fulfill. We all make mistakes and sometimes take on or promise too much. The solution is to recognize what you can realistically do and commit to that. This is a good time to change your routine, habits, or agreements.

Stage 7. *"To follow our dreams"* and pursue our need for service and creative expression, we should not neglect our other responsibilities or our own needs. This is a good time to do something creative or challenging or start a new hobby.

Stage 8. *"To follow God"* and pursue our spiritual growth, we should not neglect our need to be responsible for our family, our creative career, or the spiritual traditions we have spent a lifetime developing. By finding balance, we don't have to ring out the old to bring in the new. This is a good time to also nurture those relationships that nurture us.

Stage 9. *"To follow our destiny"* and allow life to freely unfold doesn't mean that we passively retire and let life pass us by. Instead, it is time to keep active using and growing in all of our God-given gifts and powers. This is a good time to make a commitment to help others.

Healing Our Past

To heal successfully we must satisfy our new needs without pushing away what we already have. We must remember that the urges we feel during this time are temporary and will pass as we do our best to meet them without creating chaos in our lives.

We should never trust any needs, desires, reactions, urges, cravings, compulsions, decisions, or demands that arise when we are not feeling open, loving, and centered.

We should never trust our beliefs or feelings when we are not feeling open, loving, and centered.

When our hearts are open, the unmet needs that require our attention and nurturing are real and can be wisely acted upon. When our hearts are shut down, it is not the time to make a plan for change. Our first priority must be opening our hearts to know what is the right choice for us.

9

LEARNING HOW TO
BE HEALED
AND STAY HEALED

Most approaches to healing and success focus on the teacher, the healer, the correct thinking, or the right medicine to be adopted. The nine techniques for creating practical miracles shift that focus to the student, the patient, or the client.

For example, to be healthy, a patient first needs to learn *how to be healed* and ultimately *how to stay healthy*. The patient learns how best to receive and benefit from natural healing energy. Our past overdependence on drugs, medicines, doctors, diets, and experts has created a health care crisis. Even the most conservative doctors will agree that it is unhealthy to give up responsibility for your health. Though no one will disagree with this notion, there are no real significant alternatives.

In the past, the existing medical establishment was notorious for dismissing alternative approaches, but medicine is now much more open-minded. Doctors, although still leery of severely radical practices, are embracing the importance of nutrition and other alternatives, such as chiropractic, acupuncture, and massage. It is clear that one single approach doesn't work for everyone. When various disciplines are used in tandem, healing can be more effective. Doctors are now becoming more holistic in their thinking.

Dependence on Health Care

Adults are no longer to be treated as if they are children who are incapable of choosing what works for them. Doctors don't flatly dismiss alternative options the way they used to, because if they did, they would lose patients. When doctors disapprove of alternative choices, patients go ahead anyway and experiment with them. With the vast information available on the Internet, some patients are becoming more informed than their doctors are.

Although free choice and more options are important steps, they are not the answer to the health care crisis. There is still too much emphasis on which alternative treatment or what approach can make you healthy. Whether you are dependent on doctors, shots, operations, and drugs, or lean more toward alternative approaches, you are probably still much too dependent.

Research shows that as the biggest segment of society, the Baby Boomers, ages, there is no way to satisfy its growing need for health care. We live longer now, but it is our dependence on certain expensive treatments that keeps most of us going. Relying on treatments and drugs and suffering from their side effects seriously cuts into our lifestyle, finances, and quality of life. Medicare and other government programs already are being pushed beyond their limits. Already, rising costs and an aging population are threatening the availability of quality care. Could there be another way to live longer?

We live longer today, but many of us depend on expensive treatments.

Dependence on doctors or alternative treatments is not bad or wrong. The problem is that we need them too much. We rely so much on a magic pill that we overlook our new power to heal ourselves. In being overly dependent on others, we forfeit our own self-healing power.

People today sense the possibility of staying vibrantly healthy and living a longer life, but we don't know how to get there. We sense what is possible, but we don't have the answers. This new hunger, combined with the freedom to make choices, actually increases our dependence. Real freedom, not just the freedom to choose our health care, will be experienced when we are able to use our own self-healing potential and thereby benefit from other outside treatments to accelerate our healing when necessary.

Vibrant Health

When the action of creating miracles and following your heart awakens within you the true source of happiness, then suddenly you realize how much you have been depending on food and drink to stimulate you and make you happy. This realization reveals the greatest health secret. The body becomes healthier when we are no longer dependent on food to make us happy. Suddenly, water and more simple foods become delicious. When this happens, it is easy to make adjustments in our diet without feeling in any way deprived.

**The body becomes healthier when we are no longer
dependent on food to make us happy.**

As long as you are drinking lots of water and eating
healthy foods, you can eat as much as you want and maintain your natural weight and shape. It is also not necessary
to eat healthy foods all the time. Sometimes they are just not
available. If you are healthy, occasional lapses will not affect
you adversely. Generally speaking, a good rule of thumb is
for 80 percent of your diet to consist of really healthy food
and 20 percent of it to be whatever comes your way.

Just as you can practice techniques for opening your
heart and increasing success in your life, there are also new
ways to heal your body, which use the same natural energy
that creates miracles in your life. As you give up depending
on food to be happy and recapture your natural thirst and
hunger, your body can most effectively heal itself.

The body is already perfectly designed for self-healing. In
many cases, it will do just that if we support it by providing the
necessary water, minerals, vitamins, and proteins. With these
healthy building blocks, along with your new power to create
miracles, you will be able to live a long and healthy life.

Miraculously, too, as we revert to our unique particular
shape, we begin to love ourselves more and admire the way
we look. As we begin to enjoy and appreciate our own bodies, suddenly we find that our partner's body appears more
beautiful and attractive. When we are healthy, we automatically release our unrealistic expectations of how we should
look and start to like ourselves. Self-love increases our sex
drive and increases our attractiveness to our partner.

Sex Over Forty

So many men and women over the age of forty begin to lose interest in sex. They assume this disinterest is part of growing older. They don't recognize it as a problem because they no longer feel a need. Generally speaking, we identify a problem when we are experiencing a need but can't get it satisfied.

If I want to have sex but am unable to perform, then I might consider it a problem and be motivated to do something. If I want sex and my partner is unwilling, then I would acknowledge there is a problem in the relationship and be motivated to seek help or do something to solve the dilemma. The awareness of a problem motivates us to create a solution.

Therefore, the most difficult problem to solve is one that goes undetected. If we do not feel the passionate desire for sex, then the absence of sex is not a problem. In a similar manner, as people get older, they assume that sickness is a normal part of the aging process. By making a few changes, sickness and disease lose their power over us, and we can awaken our body's natural healing capacity.

**The most difficult problem to solve
is one that goes undetected.**

Vibrant health entails not only freedom from sickness but also boundless energy. With vibrant health, living in our body becomes a huge source of pleasure. This is the gift that comes when we begin to tap into our inner creative potential.

Healing the Body, Mind, Heart, and Soul

For any miracle or positive change to take place in our life, there must be a healing on the physical, emotional, mental, and soul levels. To create miracles, we not only need to begin practicing the nine guiding principles, but must also deactivate what was holding us back as we move forward.

As we make positive changes on the physical level, we must make sure to drink more water to wash away the toxins released from our body. On an emotional level, we must learn to release old emotional issues from our past that arise. On a mental level, we must let go of limiting beliefs by exposing ourselves to new and updated beliefs. These are some examples of old beliefs versus new beliefs:

OLD BELIEF	NEW BELIEF
Change is not possible.	Miracles are now possible.
You must accept your fate.	I can create my destiny.
Don't get mad—get even.	My decisions made from kindness are more successful.
Justice must be served.	I don't depend on punishing others for relief. I am responsible for how I feel and I act from forgiveness.
Someone told me to do it.	I listen to others but follow only my heart. I—and no one else—am responsible for what I do.
Life is unfair.	I don't need to waste time dwelling on the negative because I have the power to create what I want.
You have to sacrifice to get ahead.	When I come from love, confidence, and choice, success comes to me.

Success comes from hard work.	Success comes from making decisions when I am peacefully centered in my true self.
Your childhood determines your later success.	Every moment, I have the option to connect with my unlimited potential to create what I want. My future is not determined by my past, but by what I feel, think, and do right now.
I can't make my dreams come true.	In the past I was limited, but now I can begin creating what I really want.
I shouldn't take care of my needs first.	I take care of my own needs so that I can freely give to others without strings.
I have to do it.	Based on my options, I am always free to choose what I will do and how I feel.
Something is wrong with me if I have setbacks or fear.	Setbacks and fear are a natural part of my life's journey toward increasing success.
Successful people have something I don't.	I have everything I need to create the success I want.
You owe me, and unless you pay, I can't succeed.	When I forgive the debts of others, I am freer to create the success I want.

You are responsible for my failure or loss.	There are always many factors responsible for any loss or failure. I only seek to learn a lesson and persist in creating what I want with greater wisdom.
I know my limitations.	We are living in a new age of miracles. I now have a much greater potential to create change.
That is too hard. I can't do that.	Struggle and suffering emerge when I disconnect from my power to create. As I exercise this new muscle, it will get easier.
Get married; get the love you need to be happy.	Get married to give love and not just to get love.
Spiritual development is difficult and takes years to experience.	You can feel God's energy within a few minutes of easy practice.
Romance should be automatic, and it is not supposed to last.	Romance can last, but it takes changing our ways of communicating.
Sickness is determined by our genes and age.	Genes just determine our tendency to get particular sicknesses when we disconnect from our ability to heal ourselves.
Old people automatically lose their vitality.	As we get older, we can experience vibrant health.

Reading this book and other positive inspirational books by successful people will help you release limiting beliefs from the past. But the real change occurs when we directly experience the validity of those new beliefs. Through using the nine techniques you will first activate and then begin to express your new inner potential. By healing your body, mind, heart, and spirit, you will build the foundation for creating practical miracles right away.

10

NINE TECHNIQUES FOR CREATING PRACTICAL MIRACLES

The process for creating practical miracles is tremendously accelerated when you practice the nine natural energy techniques. In any area of growing expertise, it is smart to consult the experts, learn from their experience, and test their techniques. When I wanted to learn to play the piano, I did not try to learn on my own. I found a good teacher to instruct me in his many techniques and shortcuts. When I learned to drive a car, I went to driving school. When I wanted to learn to meditate, I went to a meditation teacher. When I wanted to learn to heal, I found a great healer. Whenever we learn anything, we can benefit greatly by seeking help.

Although teachers can show us the way that has worked for them, they cannot make it work for us. After learning these new natural energy tools and techniques, it is still up to you to do the homework. In this case, I think you will find that natural energy techniques are not only helpful and relevant to your life, they are also fun. Once you get the hang of them, you can adapt them in a way that best suits you.

In this chapter, I include nine of the most powerful techniques I use to create practical miracles. They are techniques that have been developed during twenty-eight years of devoted research, study, experimentation, and testing. I have personally taught more than five hundred thousand people in my workshops and have gained tremendous results as well as the necessary feedback to refine and simplify these techniques.

These simple techniques have helped thousands of people to create practical miracles.

Many of the ideas are ancient and some are new. What is ancient and has survived through history always has value. At the same time, if an idea is ancient, in some way it probably needs a little adjusting. What is unique about the nine techniques is that they make small but significant adjustments that update ancient knowledge and skills.

These techniques do not require any particular religious belief; they support all religions. They are not a particular brand of psychology; they support all approaches. They are not medical prescriptions nor do they promise to heal, but they do facilitate your getting the most from your doctor or health care practitioner. They will assist you in awakening your power to heal yourself.

They are not a magic pill. They can do nothing and promise nothing, but they can assist you to begin creating practical miracles in your life. They teach you to drive the car, but you must be the one to get in and go.

**These techniques are not a magic pill;
you must do the homework.**

They are not necessarily better than other approaches. I share them because they work really well for me. Each person is unique. One approach may work more effectively for one person, while another may work better for someone else. I continue to learn new approaches from others and see how I can adopt what works for me and adapt what I have with new ideas and approaches. During the last thirty years, by teaching and sharing different versions of these techniques with others, I have seen them work for most.

You may find that one of these techniques works better for you than others. This is completely normal. Even for me, I have to pick and choose according to my current need or even whim. Sometimes I need one technique, while on another occasion I require a different one. To stick with a single technique would be like saying that people should eat just protein or just vegetables or just grains or just fruit or drink only water. Often we need a little of each, but at other times we may need only one.

Beginning to create practical miracles entails three requirements. First, we need to know where we are going. This insight is provided by the nine guiding principles. Even though we sometimes lose our way, if we know where we want to go, we rapidly can get back on track.

Second, we need to know what our age-appropriate needs are so we can ensure we are receiving what we specifically require while continuing to follow our hearts, conscience, duty, and dreams.

The third element is technique. To master any skill we have to practice and develop our technique. If the nine principles provide a map of where we want to go, getting what we need provides the gas. Finally, learning and practicing the nine natural energy techniques is like learning how to drive. Once you can drive, you can take off on your own.

Practicing these nine natural energy techniques, along with getting your needs met and following the nine guiding principles, opens the door for practical miracles to occur.

These new techniques don't take years of long practice to master or require any sacrifice at all. They can fit easily into anyone's life to some degree. What is really wonderful is that they work right away. One doesn't have to take it on faith that something good eventually will happen. With this immediate positive reinforcement from our daily experience, it is easier to remember to practice them. A technique can only help if we continue to use it.

Let's briefly review the nine techniques and then you can take your pick as to what you want to practice first. I suggest moving through them gradually in the order they are listed. As with all my suggestions, it is your choice what to do.

The Nine Techniques

1. By practicing the simple **Recharging Technique,** you will create the basis for making all the other techniques work more powerfully. By learning consciously to draw in natural energy, your mind will be clearer, your heart can open more, and your body will be able to get more of the vital life force it needs to be vibrantly healthy. By recharging, you can begin to accumulate more energy so that your personal charisma or magnetism increases. This increase of personal power will serve as a daily concrete experience to support the first principle of practical miracles: **Believe as if miracles are possible.**

2. The **Decharging Technique** is not only effective, but of all the techniques, it is the most fun. It just feels so good to

let the excess energy of stress or distress flow out of your body. It is wonderful to know you can do it whenever and wherever you are, in order to release your stress and burdens. For those who are more sensitive or are suffering from sickness, chronic pain, or low energy, this is often the most powerful of the nine techniques. With this new freedom for releasing the lingering effects of stress and the world, you will sigh a deep breath of relief and feel free to follow the second principle of practical miracles: **Live as if you are free to do what you want.**

3. After learning to discharge your stress, it becomes much easier to follow the **Natural Energy Diet** (see chapter 13). Much of the time our cravings for unhealthy food are an attempt to cope with stress, unhappiness, boredom, or fatigue. By having a way to release the stress pleasantly, there is no longer any great need to get energy from excess sugar or numb ourselves by overeating. As you begin the diet, you will find that your experience of energy flowing in your body is much more tangible. Discharging makes it easier to follow the diet yet the diet makes discharging more effective.

If it is difficult in the beginning to feel the energy in recharging, then practice discharging. If that is not bringing immediate results, then try going on the Natural Energy Diet for just a few days. Automatically, when you are drinking more water and eating healthy foods, you will then be able to feel the natural energy while practicing the recharging or discharging technique.

As you practice this simple and easy-to-follow diet, you will feel a greater freedom to be yourself. When you are not being tossed around by unhealthy cravings, then your soul desires can emerge. You will find that you feel young again, with so much to learn and so many places to go and enjoy. Life becomes like a toy store with endless opportunities for fulfillment and growth. You are no longer rigidly fixed, but instead are free to choose to create whatever changes you wish to make. With this freedom, you are better able to follow the third principle: **Learn as if you are a beginner.**

4. By using the **Positive Response Technique** in your relationships, at home, and at work, you will be free to let go of the past and live in present time. This allows you to stop wasting energy blaming others, feeling sorry for yourself, or blaming yourself. When you forgive others for their mistakes, then you free yourself from the tendency to become hurt, offended, and defensive. When you practice this technique to forgive others, it is really a gift to yourself. This technique gives you a way to follow the fourth guiding principle: **Love as if for the first time.**

5. By using the **Blockbuster Process** you will learn to move effortlessly through your upset feelings and come back to more positive feelings. So many times we easily can make the change if we just know what to do. By using this process you will have a map to find your way back to your true self when you feel lost. This map just assists you to look at what is true for you in any given moment, and with this increased awareness, your power to create practical miracles does the rest.

When you are upset or stuck, rather than be fooled into believing you don't have what you need to be happy, you will be able to remove the blocks within yourself. You will be free to give more of yourself rather than wait for others to give to you first. This technique gives you a way to follow the fifth guiding principle: **Give as if you already have what you need.**

6. The **Attitude Adjustment Technique** helps you to experience your ability to create results without having to do all

the work. A major element of creating success in life is coming up with the right ideas and making the right choices. By taking time to focus on your objectives and then imagining how you would feel if you had just what you wanted, then your subconscious mind has a chance to organize the best and most useful thoughts and desires. By changing your attitude about your day you can get more of what you want.

When you know what you want and you can imagine how it will feel, you are more open to recognizing the possibilities of getting there. This is in contrast to postponing feeling good until you get to where you want to go.

When we clearly experience that the feelings success can bring us are already within us right now, we can access the inner creative power that comes from feeling good rather than postponing our feeling good until some future goal is achieved. This ability to live in the moment and be motivated to create an ideal future allows us to follow the sixth guiding principle: **Work as if money doesn't matter.**

7. The **Willful Breathing Technique,** along with decharging, immediately will enrich your ability to do any of the other techniques. When nothing else works, go for a walk and breathe deeply. Walking quickly forces you to breathe, which then pumps vital oxygen into your body. Even more important to our health than water is air. We can go without water for several days, but we can't go without air for even a few minutes.

Remember, when nothing else works, take a deep breath and ask for help. When we struggle, we just have forgotten that we are not alone in this world. Support is always available. As you combine intention and breath together, you are linking up your mind, heart, body, and sprit. This technique gives you a way to follow the seventh guiding principle: **Relax as if everything will be okay.**

8. By practicing **Natural Energy Healing** you will feel a boost of spiritual energy that you did not even know was possible. When you recharge, you can pull in only the energy you can use for you, but when you heal others, you pull in much more. You can draw in what you need and what the person you are healing needs. Suddenly, God's divine or natural energy flows through you with greater power and magnitude.

If someone is receptive to healing and is very sick, then even more energy flows through, because they are so sick. Ironically, when someone is very sick or in immediate pain, you are able to feel much more energy flowing through you to heal him or her. This practical and simple-to-apply healing procedure allows you to ask for God's help to heal you as well. When you ask for healing help and you get an immediate response, it provides a strong foundation to following the eighth guiding principle: **Talk to God as if you are being heard.**

9. By practicing the **"What If" Exercise**, you will begin to experience the fact that in any moment you do have a choice about how you want to feel. So many times we are limited by our reactions, which are based on unconscious, limited beliefs from our past. When we feel blocked, sometimes we just need to reevaluate a situation from a different perspective to release that block.

By simply exploring our responses to a series of "what if" questions, we become freer to discover our true selves. With a little practice you will begin to see that in every area of your life there are limitless possibilities for you to lead a happy, healthy, rich, and fulfilled life. This is the basis for following the ninth principle: **Feast as if you can have whatever you want.**

Each of these nine different techniques for creating practical miracles is in a separate chapter. Don't attempt to learn them all at once. From this overview, get a sense of what seems interesting to you and try that first. It is too overwhelming to try to do too many things at once. All it takes to begin creating practical miracles is to start. You already have the power. Any of these techniques can work to assist you in finding that power and using it.

11

—

THE RECHARGING
TECHNIQUE

Unless you believe strongly enough to risk leaving your comfort zone to test your new creative power, you will never know you have it. If you do not believe change is possible, you will never try it. If you don't begin to use your inner potential, it can never develop and increase.

The extra energy we need to create miracles is not just present in the food we eat. It surrounds us in nature, but most of us do not know how to tap into it. When we are refreshed and rejuvenated by walking in a park, swimming in the ocean, or spending an evening sitting by a fireplace, we taste the benefits of natural energy. My experience with healing my eye is a clear demonstration of this.

By learning the simple technique of recharging, you too can learn to draw more efficiently from this energy at will from fresh air, fire, water, the earth, flowers, and from nature in general. Connecting with the natural elements not only restores our soul but also our bodies, minds, and hearts. It is literally a healing experience to stop and to smell the roses.

When inspired, happy, or energized, you are feeling the benefits of the free flow of natural energy. When stressed, pressured, anxious, or distressed, you are experiencing the symptoms of blocked natural energy. A greater awareness of pure natural energy will allow you to control it, so that when stress arrives, you quickly can return to feeling it flow.

Stress and distress are just symptoms of blocked natural energy and can be easily released.

Although the concept of drawing in energy may seem strange or foreign at first, it is actually a common experience. When you breathe in the freshness of a rose, you are naturally uplifted, because you are treating yourself to a teaspoon of natural energy. With a little practice you can learn to take in gallons of this energy every day to empower you to focus more, relax more, create more, love more, comprehend more, and enjoy more. When you stand under a shower in the morning, you are more fresh for the day, but once you learn to recharge there, your sense of rejuvenation will be that much greater.

The more directly you can feel natural energy, the more you will inhale pure positive feelings and exhale stress and distress. By practicing the simple **Recharging Technique,** you will learn not only to recognize and feel natural energy, but also to begin to accumulate it in the same way you save money in a bank. **Natural energy actually gives you the fuel to create the changes you have never before been able to make.**

To create practical miracles, we need more natural energy. The life force that permeates the universe and is always in us and around us is concentrated in each of the elements—fire, earth, air, water, and space. The refreshing feeling you get from swimming in a stream or breathing the fresh air on top of a mountain comes from pure, natural energy. When we are relaxed and surrounded by the natural elements, it is easier for us to recharge and absorb more of this precious energy.

If you are stressed, distressed, tense, or ill, you are deficient in natural energy. By learning how to absorb as much of it as possible, you can begin to relax and feel better wherever you are. It is not necessary to postpone big doses of natural energy until taking a vacation. Instead, you can create the right conditions to take in gallons of natural energy every day.

It is not necessary to wait until taking your vacation to get big doses of natural energy.

Certainly, eating good food and drinking lots of water helps, but it is not enough. By learning how to recharge, we most efficiently can absorb natural energy even when we don't have a weekend to spend in the forest or a week off to relax at the beach.

The same recharging that occurs during a great vacation can be achieved in a few minutes while standing in the shower, riding on a bus or train to work, listening to relaxing music in the car, or watching a live sporting event on TV. There is an abundance of natural energy available to us once we learn how to feel it and absorb it through our fingertips.

You can get the benefits of a great vacation by recharging for a few minutes while taking a shower in the morning.

Recharging is simple. With a little practice, you will awaken the channels in your fingertips *to sense and feel natural energy.* In the beginning, you will need to be relaxed and focused to feel it, but once you learn how, you can do it easily while watching TV or going for a walk. Any task can be difficult if we are not ready, but once we are, it becomes very easy. For a child, learning to walk is formidable until the day when he or she is ready. At that point, with a little practice, the toddler is up and moving ahead. This is the time when all of mankind can feel natural energy and learn to use it easily.

Learning to Feel Natural Energy

The first step to learning recharging is to awaken your ability to feel natural energy. To practice this simple awakening exercise, pick a time when you will not be interrupted or distracted, then follow these brief instructions. Although this experience is frequently more potent and profound when learned from a teacher or in a class, with practice, it can be experienced easily at home on your own.

The experience and description of natural energy can vary from person to person, even from time to time. Often it is a tingling feeling, similar to when your leg has "fallen asleep" and begins to wake up. At other times, it is a kind of delicate pulse or throbbing sensation. Sometimes it is warmth; sometimes it is a kind of numbness. In the more advanced stages, it is like a gentle breeze blowing into your fingertips or a current of energy that we literally are drawing in.

In the beginning, as this energy starts to flow, you occasionally may experience a sudden heaviness or a thickening of the space around you. This is a good sign that indicates that your body is experiencing a new level of energy or frequency and is adapting to integrate it.

Don't worry if the exercise doesn't work the first time, and don't give up. Remember, not everyone can throw a basketball and hit the backboard at first. To learn to hit a ball with a bat also requires several repetitions, but eventually it becomes a natural movement.

If it takes you several tries to connect to this energy, certain neural connectors in your brain still have to grow in order to make the necessary connections. Most women can do it immediately, although if a woman tends to try too hard to please others, she may need a little more practice to relax and feel the energy. If you don't feel the energy the first time, try it again after going for a brisk walk for twenty minutes. It will now be much easier to awaken this new awareness. With practice, anyone at any age can learn this process.

Feeling Natural Energy

1. For about thirty seconds, hold your hands up and simply feel your palms and fingertips while holding an imaginary basketball.

2. For about thirty seconds, while feeling your palms and fingertips, slowly pull your hands apart about six inches as if you are holding a big imaginary beach ball.

3. For about thirty seconds, while feeling your palms and fingertips, slowly bring your hands together to hold an imaginary grapefruit or orange.

4. For about thirty seconds, while feeling your palms and fingertips, pull your hands back out to hold an imaginary basketball.

5. For about the next two minutes, repeat the above four steps with your eyes closed, while practicing deliberate breathing to the count of six: six in and six out.

Once you can feel the natural energy, you literally have the power to create practical miracles at your fingertips. Next you will learn how to direct that energy as you choose.

Using Natural Energy

Natural energy responds best to your sincere and heartfelt requests. If you need more of it, it will come. Whenever you feel stressed, distressed, stuck, or sick, it is time to pull in more. Natural energy, depending on what we need in any given situation, brings greater peace, joy, confidence, love, patience, optimism, strength, humility, fulfillment, inspiration, courage, and innocence. With this kind of support, we can better focus our minds and be more creative and successful. We can open our hearts and be more loving and supportive and enjoy better communication and relationships. We literally can wash away stress and distress and feel better right away.

Natural energy is always available to respond to our needs, but we must direct it. If we don't "ask," then life proceeds as it has before, and we continue to struggle to create change all on our own without this vital help.

Natural energy is always available to respond to our needs, but we must direct it.

A request for natural energy needs to be sincere and heartfelt, not to convince the energy to respond, but to make us more receptive. A vulnerable, humble, and appreciative attitude makes you more receptive to receiving this miraculous power. To draw in more, we must always keep in mind our need for help.

This energy is not only tangible, it is intelligent. It creates our bodies, digests our foods, regulates body temperature, maintains balance and equilibrium, distributes nutrients to the billions of cells in the body, regulates breathing, keeps the heart pumping twenty-four hours a day, and contracts and relaxes muscles. It literally does everything. All we really need to do is draw it in and then direct it with our will or intention.

Preparing to Recharge

Now that you can feel the energy, the next step is to experience turning on your fingertips to direct the natural energy. Once you can direct this energy, you are ready to recharge and absorb more energy than was ever available to you before.

This introductory exercise is used solely to awaken your ability to direct energy. Once you have done it for five minutes, you are ready to practice recharging. If you are ever so stressed or distressed that it is difficult, then doing a few minutes of this warm-up exercise will prepare you to be more successful in recharging. Turning on your fingertips only takes five minutes to learn and practice.

No matter how stressed you are, turning on your fingertips only takes about five minutes.

Getting ready to recharge consists of five easy steps and two specific hand positions. Before you begin, become familiar with each of the five steps and with the two hand positions. The two hand positions are hands up and hands down. When you hold your hands up, your palms should be facing forward, fingers relaxed and pointing up, and your elbows should be relaxed at your sides. In the hands down position, your arms are at ease and extended downward. Your palms face forward and your fingers point down.

In either the up or down position, if it is more comfortable for your fingers to be slightly curled, that is fine. Over time they may naturally straighten out. Make sure they are not stiff but relaxed and comfortable. It is helpful to wiggle them occasionally to loosen up and release any rigidity or blocks. This allows the energy to flow more freely.

After becoming familiar with these two hand positions, practice moving from the up position to the down position while keeping the palms facing out. Once you are familiar with this movement, you are ready to begin.

Step 1. While standing with your hands in the down position, be aware of your fingertips. Inhale deeply to the count of six and move your hands to the up position. Make sure you inhale more deeply than you normally would. Take about three seconds to raise your hands so they rest in the up position for at least three seconds.

Step 2. While slowly exhaling to the count of six, gently lower your hands to the down position. Take about three seconds to lower them so that they rest in the down position for at least three seconds. As you move them, be aware of your fingertips.

Step 3. Repeat steps 1 and 2 ten times. Immediately before each inhale, tap the air slightly with one of your fingers. Prior to your first inhale, delicately tap the air with the little finger of your right hand. Inhale and raise your hands. Then exhale and slowly lower your hands to the down position. Then, right before the next inhale, tap the air with your next finger and then raise your hands. In this way, continue through each of your ten digits, tapping one at a time. Once you get to the thumb of your right hand, switch to your left little finger and gradually move across to your left thumb.

In this way you have repeated the up and down positions ten times and have turned on each of your fingertips. While this may seem arduous, keep in mind that it is not. It takes less than two minutes to complete ten repetitions. With a little practice, it becomes very easy. It is actually more difficult to read about than to do.

Step 4. Repeat step 3 for another ten times with an additional adjustment. Instead of merely breathing deeper, add your intention to the process verbally. Silently say to yourself the memorized intention (or MI), "Breathe in" on the inhale and "Breathe out" on the exhale. In this way, you will be connecting your will to your breath and body. For easy reference, this process of tapping each finger with one repetition of your MI is called "finger tapping."

Step 5. Now repeat step 4 another ten times with one more adjustment. Silently think of the MI "Breathe in pure positive energy" and "Breathe out stress." You will in effect be consciously directing not just your body and breath but also the natural energy. You will be drawing in fresh energy and sending out stressful energy to be recycled by nature.

To do this process effortlessly, focus on directing the energy. There is nothing else you need to do. Simply direct it and wait for it to do what it does. In the future, you will be able to turn on your fingertips easily by doing just step 5 for three cycles of ten repetitions. In a mere five minutes, your fingers will be turned on completely. Here are the five steps, in a summarized form, so that you can now look at the points and practice them at the same time:

Turning On Your Fingertips

1. Standing in the hands down position, inhale while you move into the hands up position.

2. Exhale and move to the hands down position.

3. Repeat steps 1 and 2 ten times. Count each repetition by tapping a finger before each new inhale.

4. Repeat step 3 and silently think in your mind the MI "Breathe in" on the inhale and "Breathe out" on the exhale. Remember to keep your fingers turned on with "finger tapping."

5. Repeat step 4 but silently think the MI: "Breathe in pure positive energy" and "Breathe out stress."

How to Recharge

Now you are ready to recharge. Recharging is simple. You begin by raising your hands to the up position. For the first few minutes of recharging, to activate your fingertips, or turn them on, raise your hands even higher so that your fingers are slightly above your head and your elbows are at about shoulder height. Next, repeat your MI out loud ten times with an increasing awareness of your fingertips. If it doesn't feel appropriate or comfortable to speak out loud, then thinking it is fine.

While speaking aloud the first repetition of your MI, be faintly aware of the little finger of your right hand. Before the first repetition, simply tap the finger in the air in front of it. This helps to awaken your channel so that it can draw in energy through the fingertip. In this manner, repeat your MI ten times out loud and awaken each of your fingertips. By using finger tapping, you quickly will develop the channels to receive and send energy.

After ten repetitions, while maintaining an awareness of your fingertips, begin repeating your MI silently in your mind. Take a few seconds to bring your elbows back down to a more relaxed level while maintaining the hands up position. Continue to repeat your MI silently for ten minutes.

During this process, it is normal and natural for your mind to wander and to think about other things such as shopping lists, mistakes, things you have to do, comments you or others have made, and so on. As soon as you notice your mind wandering, gently but immediately come back to repeating your MI. Once again begin to bring your awareness back to your fingertips and silently count ten repetitions with finger tapping. If there is a sudden flow of energy, you can do a shorter version. Instead of ten taps, do five. With the first repetition, tap the little finger of both hands. With the second repetition, tap the next fingers and so on.

That's all there is to it. By doing this simple technique you will begin to access a whole new level of creativity and power. You will feel more relaxed and refreshed.

Recharging gives you energy but if your body needs rest, you may get sleepy. By pulling in this energy, you will have an added edge for staying in tune with your true self. It will keep you centered so that you don't easily get swept away by reactions and cravings not in tune with what will make you healthy, happy, loving, and successful.

Picking the Right MI

Although words are not necessary, they do help us to remember our intention and assist us in creating a receptive attitude. Repeating the words "energy come" may work fine for some but for others it may not. For me, this phrase does not pull in much energy. "Energy come" tends to involve only my mind. It excludes my heart, my will, and my soul.

To pull in maximum natural energy, we need to involve all four levels of our being. Repetition creates the necessary focus, but the words we choose evoke feeling, and more feeling makes us more receptive. Ideally, what works best is using words that create a sense of sincerity, humility, vulnerability, receptivity, and confidence. For me, this MI produces that effect: "Healing Energy, I really need your help, please come, thank you."

This kind of short, heartfelt, sincere intention not only keeps my mind focused but also involves my heart, will, and soul.

If you have a particular religious preference, place at the beginning of your MI whatever name or word invokes for you a sense of spiritual reverence. If you are comfortable talking with "God," then, instead of saying "Healing Energy," you instead invite God. When I choose to recharge in a spiritual context, then my personal MI is "Oh, God, my heart is open to you, please come, sit in my heart, thank you." Here are some other examples:

"Oh, Jesus, my heart is open to you, please come, sit in my heart, thank you."

"Oh, Mother Mary, my heart is open to you, please come, sit in my heart, thank you."

"Oh, Heavenly Father, my heart is open to you, please come, sit in my heart, thank you."

"Oh, Divine Mother, my heart is open to you, please come, sit in my heart, thank you."

"Oh, Allah, my heart is open to you, please come, sit in my heart, thank you."

"Oh, Great Spirit, my heart is open to you, please come, sit in my heart, thank you."

"Oh, Krishna, my heart is open to you, please come, sit in my heart, thank you."

"Oh, Shiva, my heart is open to you, please come, sit in my heart, thank you."

"Oh, Buddha, my heart is open to you, please come, sit in my heart, thank you."

"Oh, Divine Light, my heart is open to you, please come, sit in my heart, thank you."

If you can't make up your mind, then use *"Healing Energy, I really need your help, please come, thank you."*

This usually works for everyone regardless of your spiritual background and beliefs. With a few months of practice, you will be so adept at feeling the energy that you will know what words work best for you. Once you can feel this energy, saying the prayers of your spiritual tradition will be much more powerful as well.

Setting your intention and asking for support always works, but it can help only to the extent that you can let in the support. When you can feel natural energy as you recharge, the results are much more accelerated. If your arm is under anesthesia and you cannot feel it, you cannot move it. Even if you can see it, you still cannot move it with intention. As soon as you can feel your arm, then you can move it with intention. Likewise, when you can feel the divine energy, you can pull in God's many blessings.

Understanding the Principle of Resonance

Now that you are able to recharge or draw in natural energy through your fingertips, you can secure the greatest amount of energy by surrounding yourself with the natural elements. When you recharge, experiment by doing it while feeling the influence of water, fire, air, earth, and space. Keep in mind that it is not precisely the elements that provide you with energy. They merely assist you in tuning in to the frequency of the natural energy that is always around you in endless supply.

All energy travels in waves or frequencies, and each element has its own frequency band. Recognizing and enjoying a particular element opens our minds and hearts to the natural energy resonant with the element. Through this process of resonance, we begin to pull it in.

When a C note is played on the piano and a guitar is nearby, the guitar string automatically will begin to resonate and make a C sound. In a similar manner, as you feel natural energy, you can begin to resonate with all the frequencies of nature and open yourself to increasing your access to it.

In a sense, each element is like a particular channel on TV. All of the stations are always being broadcast. When we turn to a new channel, we are just picking a different frequency. When you pick up on that frequency, you are not draining the broadcasting station. The frequencies are always being sent out regardless of whether or not they are being picked up.

Each element is a new channel for us to pick up a different frequency of positive energy.

When an element is rich and vibrant in pure natural energy, then that particular frequency is awakened in you and you can begin to access its energy. A fresh rose, for example, is one of the most healing frequencies in nature. Even without an awareness of natural energy, practically anyone can be uplifted when they smell the freshness of a rose. When you learn to recharge near freshly cut roses or hold a couple of roses in your hands, you can awaken your body's natural healing power dramatically.

To find comfort, we are automatically attracted to situations that include the elements we need most. Some people love to sit in the sun, while others enjoy long showers. This often is because one soul needs more fire energy while another requires more water energy. As a young boy, I always wanted to sit by the heater; this was my need for fire energy. Later in my life, I loved taking long showers; this was motivated by my need to draw in the water energy.

We tend to be attracted to situations that include the elements we need most.

When our hearts are open we are attracted to what we need, but when our hearts are closed, we are repelled by the elements we need most. For example, when you are depressed you may dread going for a walk in nature when that is just the thing you need to do. If you are really stressed, then the thought of recharging is also repelling. Fortunately it is so easy and adaptable that you can do it in any situation without any effort. Because it works so quickly, your heart opens again, and you are able to appreciate the natural energy that you need.

To make use of an element, you can simply recharge near it or feel or enjoy its influence in some way. For example, to recharge with the sun, sit in the rays of the rising or setting sun. To recharge with water, drink lots of water, lay in a bath, or stand in a shower. The process of recharging and decharging is explored with additional detail in my book *How to Get What You Want and Want What You Have.*

12

THE DECHARGING TECHNIQUE

Only when you follow your heart, not the rules of others, can you grow up and realize your miraculous inner power. You can only create miracles when you are in the driver's seat. Be true to yourself, and the truth will come to you. Don't let trying to be "good" or focusing only on pleasing others keep you from following your inner free will. You can't please everyone, so don't even try.

At the same time, don't allow your reactions to keep you from expressing who you truly are. As you assert yourself in confidence and complete freedom, be careful simply not to rebel, defy, or react. Instead, let your actions and choices reflect your true considerate, compassionate, wise, and patient self.

Real freedom comes when we are free of addictive cravings and reactions. So many times in life we know something is not right for us, yet we do it anyway. The craving is so intense that we just can't resist. It is unnatural to thirst for that which is not what we need. Doing so disconnects us from our inner potential. By learning to awaken our true needs and desires, we are able to free ourselves from unhealthy reactions, compulsions, cravings, and addictions.

To remain connected to our true self, who is confident, joyful, peaceful, and loving, we must learn how to release stress and distress. Just as a car accumulates dirt and grime, so does our soul after a while. Just as you can recharge with positive energy, you can learn to decharge stress and distress. With a variety of easy-to-practice **Decharging Techniques**, by consciously using natural elements, you will learn to feel better immediately.

Once you have practiced recharging, you can begin decharging right away. For many people in the West, this technique is even more powerful than recharging. Decharging allows you to relax and release stress and distress, so that you feel better and can absorb more positive energy by recharging. When we are stressed, pressured, distressed, and so on, our energy is blocked in some way. This restriction creates a buildup of energy and hence we may feel like we want to explode. Through decharging you can release this excess energy without having to explode at others. All addictions are just unhealthy ways to release excess energy. Decharging is a healthy way to do the same thing. As you practice decharging, it is easy to give up addictions and minimize emotional ups and downs.

Although it is a common experience, most people are unaware that, in addition to absorbing positive energy from others, we can absorb stress and distress. Children absorb a lot of their parents' stress, distress, even their pain. Unless the parents are able to handle their problems responsibly, their children often absorb these negative emotions. This tendency to take on the stress, distress, and pain of others continues into adulthood. To combat it, we have to become less concerned about pleasing others, but we also have to learn to decharge the unresolved stress, distress, and pain from our past.

Children absorb a lot of their parents' stress, distress, and even their pain.

By releasing stress and then absorbing more positive energy you will become less affected by the stress of others. Quite often, one of the major causes of cancer and other life-threatening diseases is the absorption of stress. When medicine cannot help a situation, it is usually because the person's own healing power is blocked by accumulating too much stress and distress over the years. Much of this stress was not even originally their own.

Unless we learn to decharge our stress by sending out excess energy and then filling up with fresh new natural energy, our bodies tend to get sick. A vast majority of ill-nesses are complicated by our lack of water to wash away toxins, but they are also affected by our inability to let go of past stress and distress. By learning to decharge, people are more effectively able to heal themselves.

After we decharge, it is good to fill up again and recharge for a few minutes.

When I finally learned to decharge, an enormous weight was lifted from my shoulders. I was finally able to use the many natural elements more efficiently to dispense with accumulated stress.

Understanding the Natural Flows of Energy

Being a loving and giving person not only feels good but gives us energy. At the same time, it makes us vulnerable to picking up more stress and distress. This is not a problem if we continue to fill up with positive energy and are able to send back into nature any excess energy.

When we help others who are stressed or distressed, we may also receive some of their stress and distress. Any time you help someone, there is always an exchange of energy. By being in a supportive relationship, you are able to pull in more positive energy. However, if you happen to have less stress than another does, you will absorb part of their stress and distress as well. As they feel better from interacting with you, their stress lifts out of them and part of it travels to you.

Besides getting positive energy when we help others, we also get a little of their stress and distress.

This is a simple exchange, just like the exchange between heat and cold. A warm room gets cooler and a cool room gets warmer when the door between them is opened. All people who gain fame or notoriety are affected in this way. When a singer like Barbra Streisand enchants her audience, her fans' hearts begin to open and their stress is released. A part of this stress goes to Barbra.

Unless she is prepared for this by having support in her life to release this added stress, she will begin to suffer problems. Her normal little problems or stresses in life will suddenly seem bigger and more gripping. This simple insight explains why fame is like putting a huge magnifying glass up to our every shortcoming and limitation.

At work, unless we are regularly able to release the stress we accumulate, we will eventually get sick or burn out. Giving to others nourishes our spirit until we begin absorbing so much stress that we become blocked from receiving the energy we need. To avoid burnout, we must make sure we are doing what we want to be doing and be aware that, as the stress accumulates, we need to find a way to release it.

When you are upset, stressed, or distressed, you are generally just overcharged with energy. The process of decharging sends out excess energy so that your upset becomes more manageable. When it is difficult to resolve upset feelings and we can't just let go of them, it automatically becomes easier if we send out excess energy. Don't feel concerned that you will lose energy. You are only sending out excess energy. Once you have sent out the excess energy, then it is easier to come back to feeling peaceful, joyful, confident, and loving.

The process of decharging sends out excess energy so that your upset becomes more manageable.

Even when we absorb a lot of positive energy, it may activate or charge up little issues and make them bigger than we can handle. Have you ever noticed that at special occasions, when there is always a lot of energy and love, you may easily become upset or overwhelmed? This means that you just need to decharge this stress by sending out some excess energy. Let Mother Nature help you out by taking a little of that energy that is overwhelming and upsetting you.

Usually when we absorb a lot of energy we collect some stress as well. Stress makes us contract; thus, the more stress we absorb, the less energy we can handle. By sending out excess energy, we can then become more centered, and, as a result, receive even more energy through recharging. After decharging it is fun and energizing to recharge for a few minutes and see how much more positive energy we can handle.

Sometimes in the beginning people don't feel the flow of

energy through using the recharging technique. In some cases, it is because they have been so open to absorbing stress that to protect themselves from getting sick, they have closed up. They just can't handle any more energy. For these people, by first starting to send the energy out, they can begin to relax again and then they fill back up with energy. By decharging first, they can then benefit from recharging.

By first sending out excess energy, some people can then fill back up with more energy.

You can never recharge too much. Recharging does not produce excess energy. When you are full, it just stops working until you use up some of that energy. We get excess energy through sharing our energy and then having more come back to us. In a very real sense, when you give your love and support to others, more energy comes back to you. When you give a lot, you will end up with excess energy. At this point you need to decharge.

This helps explain why many people get really sick with life-threatening diseases like cancer. Many very sick people tend to be loving people who give a lot and absorb a lot of stress and distress from others. Repeatedly, I have witnessed accelerated recovery with cancer patients and many other sicknesses and disease through decharging. Excess energy is clearly a major contributing factor to chronic pain and sickness. Even chronic fatigue is the result of excess energy. Although this seems paradoxical, it is easy to comprehend. We feel energized when our energy is flowing. Fatigue comes from blocked energy. Excess energy results when energy flow is blocked. Besides causing stress, distress, fatigue, and pain, with excess energy the body loses its ability to heal itself. Instead of naturally healing a sickness, the body gets weaker and weaker until it develops a life-threatening sickness.

When you send excess energy back into nature, it is like giving nature fertilizer. The movement of the energy from you to a natural element transforms the stressful vibrations. If, however, you send too much energy into a flower, for example, it may begin to droop because it now has excess energy. Remember: You are not sending stress into a natural element but just the excess energy that is making you more stressed.

Stress, distress, fatigue, and pain only result when your energy is blocked by negative beliefs or attitudes. When you relax back to feelings like understanding, forgiveness, appreciation, and trust, then the stress disappears. Stress is like darkness. You cannot make it go away. All you can do is turn on the light. With understanding, forgiveness, and other positive feelings, we automatically dispel the darkness of stress.

Stress is like darkness.
You cannot make it go away.
All you can do is turn on the light.

This process of dispelling the darkness of stress is very difficult when we are experiencing excess energy. By sending out the energy, we can then easily release our stress, distress, resistance, and pain. Without excess energy to deal with, when you absorb a little stress you can easily transform it back to peace and relaxation. Releasing excess energy makes stress, distress, and so on, easily processed or managed by you.

If you are suffering from a really hot day, then, to cope better, you go and take a shower and cool down. Then you can go back out and deal with the heat again. If you are upset, by taking a few deep breaths you can cool down and be more centered. In both examples, taking a shower or taking a few deep breaths are simple discharging techniques. In a similar way, when life is really stressful, by releasing the blocked or excess energy, you can relax and then once again go back and interact from a more centered perspective.

Imagine energy could be explained in terms of watts like different sizes of light bulbs. If you have one hundred watts of peaceful energy and you absorb from the outer world two hundred watts of stressful energy, then clearly you will begin to resonate with the stressful energy and feel stressed.

But if you had two hundred watts of peaceful energy and absorbed one hundred watts of stressful energy, then it would not affect you much. Still, having that excess energy would make you feel some increased stress.

If you had two hundred watts of peaceful energy and absorbed two hundred watts of peaceful energy, but you could only handle two hundred watts, then you would begin to feel really stressed. Little things that would not normally bother you would suddenly become big issues. Excess energy is the number one reason we overreact to situations.

In each of the three above examples, decharging will help lessen the energy level so that you can easily manage your stress. Decharging is the ultimate stress-management technique.

**Decharging is the ultimate
stress-management technique.**

Decharging is not a big job. It is just making your recreation time more efficient in reducing your stress levels and generating happiness. Hopefully, this information will motivate you to take more time to enjoy and relax in nature. With this new insight, connecting with nature is not a luxury for the rich, but a necessity for increasing success, lasting love, and vibrant health.

Never use this information to be afraid of stress or other people's stress levels. Just as you can absorb stress in a few minutes, you can also release it in a few minutes. The more sensitive you are, the more you will tend to gather stress. This is not a problem because if you can absorb it easily, then you can also discharge more easily. Accumulating stress only becomes a problem when you don't take time to discharge.

Now, next time you feel pressured, burdened, stressed, or overwhelmed, you will recognize that you have absorbed too much energy and it is time to discharge. It doesn't matter whether you absorb peaceful, loving energy or stressed energy: when it is too much energy, then you become stressed.

The stress of others makes you feel stressed only when it is too much energy for you to handle. There are many times when you can handle the stress of others. At those times, you are absorbing stress but you have enough peaceful positive energy to transform it. We become stressed when the stress absorbed is greater than the peace we have. So, don't be afraid of stress, but recognize that it can make you stressed or even sick if you don't take time to discharge.

How to Discharge

Discharging is easily learned in three stages. Please don't be in a hurry to do the more advanced stages. Give yourself at least a few weeks of practice for each stage. These are the three stages:

Stage 1

The procedure for discharging is very similar to recharging. You repeat your recharging memorized intention (MI) about ten times in the hands-up position to turn on your fingertips. Then move your hands to the hands-down position in the presence of some natural element and repeat your selected discharge memorized intention (MI).

To create a discharge MI, simply add another phrase to your usual recharge MI. Here is an example:

Healing Energy,
I really need your help.
Please come.
Take away my excess energy,
Thank you.

By adding "Take away my excess energy," it becomes
quite amazing. Suddenly, the energy flow changes and you
can feel energy flowing out of your fingertips. As the energy
flows, feel free to adjust your hand position. It may be that
letting them relax by your side increases the flow or it may
work better for you by pointing your fingers in the direction
of the source of natural energy.

Once you have picked a memorized intention for decharging that feels comfortable, stick with it for many weeks. By
using the exact words each time, the process will be more automatic and more effective.

When it is automatic, then you can easily hold in the back
of your mind a clear idea of the issue you want decharged
while you repeat the MI. Being aware of the upset feelings or
reactions that you want to decharge makes decharging even
more powerful. You don't have to know what is bothering
you, but the more aware you are of what you want decharged
the more efficient the process is.

Stage 2

Once you get the hang of Stage 1, then you are ready for
Stage 2. In his stage, make your request more precise and
therefore more efficient. After inviting the natural energy,
then take a moment to acknowledge the simple truth that
you know the element contains natural energy. In addition,
instead of using the phrase "Take away my excess energy,"
become more specific and use a phrase like, "Use this fire to
burn my excess energy."

In Stage 2 the decharge MI would be the following:

Healing Energy,
I really need your help.
Please come.
I know you are in this fire.
Use this fire to burn my excess energy,
Thank you.

By making this small adjustment and by making your intention more specific, more of your mind, heart, and intention become involved in the decharging process.

"I know you are in this fire" engages your mind more.

"Use this fire" connects your will or intention to the fire.

"Burn my excess energy" rather than the generic phrase "Take away my excess energy" makes the request more poetic and descriptive and thus involves your heart more.

These two adjustments in Stage 2 allow you to connect and resonate more fully with the natural healing energy in the fire. A similar adjustment can be made in dealing with whatever element you choose. Here are a few examples:

Healing Energy,
I really need your help.
Please come.
I know you are in this water.
Use this water to wash away my excess energy
Thank you.

Healing Energy,
I really need your help.
Please come.
I know you are in this earth.
Use this earth to draw out my excess energy.
Thank you.

Healing Energy,
I really need your help.
Please come.
I know you are in this fresh air.
Use this air to take away my excess energy.
Thank you.

Healing Energy,
I really need your help.
Please come.
I know you are in this space.
Use this space to absorb my excess energy.
Thank you.

Healing Energy,
I really need your help.
Please come.
I know you are in these beautiful roses.
Use these roses to take away my excess energy.
Thank you.

Healing Energy,
I really need your help.
Please come.
I know you are in this beautiful music.
Use this music to dissolve my excess energy.
Thank you.

Healing Energy,
I really need your help.
Please come.
I know you are in this refreshing lavender scent.
Use this lavender scent to absorb my excess energy.
Thank you.

Healing Energy,
I really need your help.
Please come.
I know you are in this pleasing sensation.
Use this massage to absorb my excess energy.
Thank you.

Healing Energy,
I really need your help.
Please come.
I know you are in this delicious food.
Use this food to draw out my excess energy.
Thank you.

Healing Energy,
I really need your help.
Please come.
I know you are in this gold.
Use this gold to neutralize my excess energy.
Thank you.

Use any of the above specific phrases to generate the desired flow of energy. Once the flow is occurring, you can shorten the MI. For example,

Healing Energy in this fire,
please burn my excess energy.
Thank you.

Here is another example of a short MI:

Healing Energy,
use your beautiful roses to take away my excess energy.
Thank you.

As a general guideline, use the longer MI at least ten times before using the shorter MI. If your mind wanders, or the energy flow lessens, then come back to the longer MI.

How to Use the Five Elements

When using the fire element you can use a fireplace, the rays of the sun in the early morning and at sunset, or simply a candle. Light bulbs, however, don't work. Decharging under the full moon is one of the most powerful ways to open the heart.

When using the earth element, you can use the ground, big rocks, crystals, trees, gardens, grass, and basically anything that grows in nature. Flowers tend to be the most powerful dechargers for serious illnesses or emotional distress. Gold, diamonds, and other precious stones tend to be very powerful elements for decharging.

When using the air element, it is best to use fresh air. To increase your ability to decharge using air, do it while going on a walk or while exercising. Stagnant air can only absorb so much excess energy and that is why fresh air is recommended. Even in the wintertime it is good to open the windows for five to ten minutes to freshen the room.

When using the water element, you can use a bathtub, pool, hot tub, or shower. You can even decharge into a glass of water and then drink it. It will continue to decharge you as it moves through your body. You can be in the water or just standing near it. The best water decharge is near or in a river, lake, or ocean.

When using the space element, you can decharge in the presence of or within a large space, a vista view, a holy place, a power place, a healing springs, a big dome ceiling, or any space that inspires you. Burning pleasing incense or smoke that permeates space can also be used to decharge.

All things that are healing, inspiring, nurturing, or relaxing can be used to decharge. Some common examples are the healing sensation of massage, the different healing scents of aromatherapy, the different healing herbs and homeopathic remedies, pleasing music and dance, as well as delicious food.

Whatever medicine, tonic, or remedy you take you can also use it to decharge before you take it.

The more you work with one element, the more connected you will become to that element. By taking a month to really focus on one particular element, your effectiveness in decharging will increase. In the beginning, test the different elements and see what works best for you and then focus for at least a month primarily on that element; then you are ready to do the same with the other four. There is no right order or time period for everyone.

If you don't know where to start, then, if you are a feeling-type person, start with water. If you are a more physical person, start with the earth. If you are a mental person, start with the air. And, if you are intuitive, go with fire.

If your blocks are jealousy, judgment, or resentment, work with fire. If your blocks are depression, procrastination, self-pity, then work with earth. If your blocks are confusion, indecision, anxiety, then work with air. If your blocks are indifference, perfectionism, or guilt, then work with water.

If you want more peace, patience, and fulfillment, then work with fire. If you want more joy, optimism, and inspiration, then work with earth. If you want more confidence, strength, and courage, then work with air. If you want more love, humility, and innocence, then work with water.

You can use space to decharge all the blocks and generate all the positive feelings. With space, these healing frequencies can be generated, but they are not as grounded as with the other elements and therefore not as practical for healing stress and distress. The space element is best, however, for having spiritual experiences or connecting more with our inner potential.

Stage 3

When decharging becomes easy and automatic, then you can add even another phrase that briefly describes the condition you want decharged. In Stages 1 and 2 it was important to have a sense of what you wanted to decharge. In this stage, your request becomes more precise and you state exactly what you want decharged.

Each of the three stages adds a little more precision. Learning to decharge needs to be in stages because too much precision makes the process too mental and not easy and comfortable. Only proceed to this stage when Stage 2 is easy and comfortable.

In this stage, add a simple phrase to very briefly put in words what you want to decharge. For example, "Decharge my disappointment" or "Decharge my anger." When you are stressed or distressed it is most effective to decharge emotions that you can feel. If you clearly feel the emotion then it is much easier to decharge.

It would not work as well to say, "Decharge whatever anger I have"; instead it works better to say, "Decharge my anger." As you think this phrase, try to feel your anger a little more intensely. Let it build up as you continue to decharge it, and then it will just disappear or become easy to release. You could even say, "Decharge my anger about this work situation." Be precise but keep it real simple.

A really old-fashioned way to deal with anger was to go start a war and get in a fight. By expressing the excess energy that fuels the anger, it goes away, and then people make up. War, fighting, and yelling is really just an out-of-date way of decharging.

This explains why male teenagers after getting in fights would then become close friends. By fighting they would release the excess energy and then be able to make up or create peace.

Couples often make up after a yelling fight not because they have really resolved anything, but they have just used up their excess energy fighting and then forget what they were fighting about. Usually we can't even remember what we are fighting about even during a fight. Once the excess energy is out, their energy can freely flow again and they enjoy passionate sex.

The problem with fighting to release excess energy is that every time our energy becomes excess, we pick another fight until we just close down and don't let more energy in. Learning to discharge helps you establish healing and harmonious ways to release excess energy and stop fighting.

Most compulsive habits or reactions that we have difficulty changing continue to occur because we have excess energy and no other way to release it. We do things we regret and then resolve later to not do it again. Yet we do it again and again. Why? Because that activity in some way burns up our excess energy and gives us temporary relief.

Smoking, drinking alcohol, overeating, coffee, and refined sugar and overprocessed carbohydrates all give us relief because in some way they burn excess energy. They would be great for us if they didn't also stress our bodies in some way. These substances are not bad in themselves but become harmful when they are used in excess. Generally speaking, everything in moderation is fine.

When discharging stress, distress, pressure, and pain it is best to be fully feeling it at the time and more precisely feeling the emotions associated with the stress, distress, and so on. The twelve most potent healing emotions for discharging are anger, sadness, fear, sorrow, frustration, disappointment, worry, embarrassment, rage, hurt, panic, and shame.

Here is an example of a Stage 3 discharge MI:

Healing Energy,
I really need your help.
Please come, *discharge my anger*.
I know you are in this fire.
Use this fire to burn my excess energy,
Thank you.

Using the Blockbuster Chart in chapter 15 you can determine what emotions you need to discharge in order to best remove one of your blocks. Sometimes it is hard to determine what emotion is underlying your stress. In this case just go down the list and try each one until something clicks and you begin to feel the flow of energy. At this point you will begin to feel the underlying emotion intensify before it lessens and disappears.

If you wish to be more precise, you can work with certain elements to discharge certain emotions. Fire best discharges anger, frustration, and rage. Earth best discharges sadness, disappointment, and hurt. Air best discharges fear, worry, and panic. Water best discharges sorrow, embarrassment, and shame. Space can discharge all the emotions but not as deeply as the more dense elements of fire, earth, air, and water.

It is my hope that this simple technique be taught to patients seeking a more speedy recovery from sickness. Through learning this simple but powerful tool, any person can share responsibility for their healing and not just depend on their doctors for treatment. Not only will they heal faster but they will have learned how to stay healthy as well.

Through decharging we automatically awaken our body's capacity to heal itself. This awakening increases the recovery period in healing any and every disease. It does not, however, replace the need for outside help.

Whether you are sick, stressed, or upset, decharging can immediately start giving you the relief you are looking for. Even business deals work better when you practice decharging. When you feel peaceful and relaxed while also enthusiastic and motivated, people naturally want to cooperate with you.

Ultimately, decharging allows you to be your authentic self without having to get lost overreacting to life's restrictions and limitations. With this freedom to be yourself you will find increasing power to create practical miracles in your life.

13

THE NATURAL
ENERGY DIET

To learn as if you are a beginner, open your mind and heart and continue to grow at all times. Learn from the experts but don't give away your power. Although your mind and heart are open like a child's, remember that you are not a beginner in life. No one but you knows what is best for you, and only you can know that in your heart. To grow in life, it is essential to continue to learn from others and their experiences, but we must always follow our own consciences.

On the other hand, when we think we know it all and don't need others, we unintentionally hold ourselves back from change. If you are not making all your dreams come true, then you clearly need help. The form of that help is your choice. There is no shame in needing help. That is why we are all here on earth together. Now, more than at any time in history, there is so much available knowledge and expertise. Go into any bookstore or go online, and you have immediate access to the greatest experts of all times.

By understanding the underlying reasons people get sick, you can learn how to maintain vibrant health along with the strength and stability to create increasing success and lasting love. With a clear understanding of how you contribute to your limitations, you then can begin to make a positive change. Ultimately, this strength and clarity can be lived only when your body is healthy or on the way to becoming so.

Once you have learned to discharge your stress, it becomes easy to follow the **Natural Energy Diet**. You will begin to feel naturally peaceful, energized, and more grounded. You will be able to face life's challenges in a manner so easy that you never dreamed it would be possible. From this secure foundation, you will be able to contact your true desires, risk change, then follow through to success, bolstered by the increased energy of your inner passion.

To benefit from the healing that occurs from recharging and discharging, it is essential that we drink lots of water. This is the basis of the Natural Energy Diet. If we are raising our energy level in order to be more successful, loving, and healthy, then inevitably we will attract and absorb stress and distress. If you wear a white suit on a camping trip, it will get dirty. When your heart is open to the world, even if you establish healthy boundaries, you still will absorb some stress and distress. When a person rises up to be a leader, their very presence uplifts others and, as a result, he or she absorbs some of his or her followers' stress and distress.

For this reason influential people sometimes get sick or suffer huge mood swings. With awareness, these problems can be solved by regularly discharging this accumulating stress and distress. When this energetic purification occurs, the release of stress must occur on the physical level as well.

Whenever any purification occurs on the soul, mental, and emotional levels, toxins automatically are released into the body and must be eliminated. Unless we are drinking more water to wash away toxins, the positive changes we make in our mind, heart, and soul cannot be sustained.

To sustain good health, the body requires about a half gallon of water a day. More precisely, a healthy body daily requires a half ounce of water for every pound. For example, if you weigh 128 pounds, then you need 64 ounces or a half gallon of water a day, or eight 8-ounce glasses of water. If you drink more than 4 ounces of water every twenty minutes, then it's good to add a pinch of sea salt to the water. Other liquids do not fulfill this need. If, however, you are purifying stress, distress, resistance, or sickness, the body needs twice as much water, or a minimum of one gallon of water a day. If you happen to exercise and perspire, then you will need even more. If you drink a gallon of water a day, whenever possible, mix in a little sea salt. Too much water can wash away electrolytes. Mix one teaspoon of sea salt with a gallon of water or just put a pinch of sea salt, when available, in your glass.

In some cases of healing sickness, if a gallon of water a day is not sustained, the toxins released can temporarily intensify one's symptoms. Even if people go on a healing diet, unless they drink more water to release the toxins, the new healthy diet can feel like torture. When the diet is over, they will binge.

People who diet will later binge, because they are not also discharging and drinking more water.

For this reason, once you start discharging and drinking more water to wash away released toxins, you easily can make a few important dietary changes. The first and most important change is to increase natural foods and remove refined and processed foods from the diet. Natural food is food that hasn't been processed to increase its shelf life in the store. Foods that will spoil right away are always the easiest for your body to digest and assimilate nutrition from.

The most important food to replace is refined sugar. This doesn't mean you have to give up desserts forever. The idea is first to give up your sugar addiction so that you can feel your natural hunger once again. Then eat occasional desserts in moderation and only if you are at your healthy weight.

When you feel natural hunger, you don't experience an unnatural addictive craving for sugar and other foods that are not good for your body. When I learned how to replace sugar with an abundance of natural foods, I began effortlessly losing extra weight at the rate of one pound every few days. After losing thirty pounds in eight weeks, I got back my natural, healthy shape. As a result, I now feel light, healthy, and strong. Drinking a gallon of water a day, along with decharging, makes it easy to give up refined sugar. Once you are back to health, it is fine to come back to a half gallon of water a day as a minimum. When you are back to feeling natural thirst, then you will know how much more to drink. When you experience increased stress or distress in your life, then automatically you will thirst for more than a half gallon a day.

When you stop eating refined sugars (fruits, however, are fine), immediately your body rejoices and begins to heal itself by releasing old toxins. If you don't supply enough water for your body to wash away these toxins, then very quickly your body becomes blocked and murky with toxins. This lowers your energy, and suddenly you feel a craving for the quick energy you get from refined sugars. By drinking one gallon of water a day, your sugar cravings are easily replaced by healthy desires for natural fruit or honey. Artificial sweeteners are unhealthy and should be avoided like rat poison.

**To lose excess weight and be healthy, the most
important food to replace is refined sugar.**

The Natural Energy Diet is simple. Eat more good and
healthy foods. Don't ever go on a crash or fad diet. Eat as
much as you want of the foods that you like. Eating amply is
essential to maintaining your normal body size. Research
has shown that when dieters deprive themselves, they gain
back the lost weight or more and then have even greater difficulty losing it. That is because the body experiences the
deprivation as famine and holds on to all its available fat.

Create plentiful food with lots of menu choices. Though
some people need only two or three meals a day, others need
many little meals every so often throughout the day. The
secret of the Natural Energy Diet is to eat whenever you are
hungry and as much as you want. This principle works once
you are in touch with your natural thirst and hunger. If you
are still addicted to sugar, you will be driven to eat all the
wrong foods for your body. Unless you are first in touch
with your natural thirst and hunger, eating what you want is
like wandering through the streets of New York blindfolded.

What I mean by "good and healthy" foods is generous serv-
ings of grains, legumes, beans, proteins, potatoes, vegetables
(both raw and lightly cooked), fruits and dried fruits, nuts,
unprocessed oils, unrefined or unleavened breads, and even
some dairy products, if your body can tolerate them. Eat lots
of potatoes. Use an abundance of these healthy foods to
replace refined and processed foods. Try to avoid eating too
much of a single food or food group. By consuming a large
variety of foods, you will discover that your natural hunger is
appropriately stimulated.

**Create lots of food around you with
lots of choices of things to eat.**

What makes this diet easy to follow is that you don't have to do it all the time for it to work. If you are reasonably healthy, you can follow it 80 percent of the time to reap its full benefit. There is no advantage to striving for perfection. Once you are healthy and at your healthy weight, you can eat junk food 20 percent of the time. Whenever you have a choice, go for the healthy food. Eat the junk only when you are hungry and nothing healthy is available. If you find that you are craving junk food, then avoid that food for a few weeks and go back to drinking a gallon of water a day. Please keep in mind that before beginning any new dietary program, if you are sick it is wise to consult with a medical expert who is familiar with your body's specific needs.

**Once you are healthy and strong, it is okay to make
junk food 20 percent of your diet.**

Your natural hunger can be awakened only after you feel your natural thirst. This is the most important step. Just for one month, eat as much as you want, but give up all liquids except water, and make sure that you drink at least a gallon a day. Avoid ice-cold water, as it puts an added strain on the body. Room-temperature water or herbal tea is ideal. Avoid fruit juices as well. Although they are not refined sugar, they are too concentrated and will prevent you from awakening your natural thirst. Drinking only plain water for a month is the most powerful dietary change you will ever make, and it is easy. Within weeks you will begin to experience what most of us have forgotten: real and natural thirst. With this program your natural hunger will begin to develop, and you will want those healthy foods rather than the fast-burning refined sugars, breads, and pastries.

Once you have established this healthy baseline, it is easy to come back into healthy balance. If no good, healthy, and wholesome food is readily available, eat what foods you can find and then remember to drink at least a gallon of water a day for the next few days afterward. To compensate for eating junk food, make sure you follow up with really healthy food. This kind of balance is all that is required to experience vibrant health. As a basic rule of thumb, whenever you drink something that is off the diet, including beer, alcohol, wine, juice, coffee, or any nonherbal stimulant, then follow up by drinking a glass of water to dilute it.

Not only do caffeine and alcohol overstimulate your body, but they also dehydrate you. The main reason people suffer from hangovers is that they are dehydrated. By drinking one glass of water for every alcoholic beverage you consume, your body more easily can cope with the indulgence. In addition, whenever you eat, it is fine to drink water. Particularly if you are eating junk food, make sure you drink a glass of water along with it.

Keep in mind that if you do vigorous exercise or perspire heavily, your body requires more salt and water. A jogger, for example, needs at least an extra half to a gallon of water. One of the reasons regular exercise can make people healthy is that it allows them to breathe more fully and motivates them to drink more water.

Increasing your intake of salt is an important part of the Natural Healing Diet. Throughout history, salt always has been valued for its healing properties and often literally was worth its weight in gold. Doctors recently have retracted their incorrect conclusions that salt is not good for you. Sea salt is even healthier than iodized salt. Put as much as you like on your food. Yet certain health conditions may require you to give up salt, so check with your doctor.

Replacing refined sugar, apart from drinking more water, is the most critical aspect of this diet. When your body digests refined sugar, in order to create the sudden burst of energy or "sugar high," it leaches precious minerals out of the body. After removing toxins, rebuilding the body with minerals is the next most important element in healing. Unless our bodies contain sufficient minerals, they cannot heal or sustain positive changes in our mind, heart, and soul.

After removing toxins, rebuilding the body with minerals is the next most important element in healing.

Most of our food, unless organically grown, is already mineral deficient. One of the main benefits of organic produce is that the soil is cared for in a way that increases the mineral content of the food. The power of natural healing energy is blocked when minerals are depleted from the body. Minerals are essential for conducting the natural energy flow throughout the body as well as serving as important tools for rebuilding the body. Liquid mineral supplements are available everywhere and are very helpful.

Restoring Your Natural Thirst and Hunger

It usually takes about four weeks to restore your body's natural thirst and hunger. To do this, try to be on the Natural Energy Diet 100 percent of the time. The first four weeks is the only period in which you have to be so strict with yourself. Just do it once, and you will lose all or much of your excess weight and heal certain conditions that just wouldn't go away previously. Most important, you will become free of your addictive cravings.

To begin this change, make sure you are surrounded by lots of really good food. By drinking a gallon of water a day, you will discover that your old sugar cravings miraculously go away. Drink *at least* a gallon a day, keeping in mind that the more water you drink, the better. Replace all fluids with water and satisfy your sweet tooth with fresh or dried fruit.

Once you begin regularly decharging and drinking a gallon of water a day, making these changes is easy. At the end of the four weeks, you will want to stay on the diet. This is fine, as long as you don't stress out about it. Figuring out how to get healthy food all the time actually can cause enhanced stress and distress. A diet that is 80 percent ideal is a good goal almost anyone can achieve. Once you are healthy and back to your ideal weight, then it is only necessary to drink a half gallon of water a day.

During these four weeks you will be detoxifying your body. The toxins that emerge are those responsible for your unnatural cravings. As they leave the body, you may start to crave sugar or unhealthy foods. At these times, simply drink a glass of water, then practice decharging with air or fire. Breathing exercises or vigorous walking can be very helpful to burn off the stress and distress being released.

When you crave refined sugar, avoid fruit juices, but eat lots of whole fruit, nuts, and dates. They are great replacements for candy bar addicts. In just a few days, you will have regained your natural thirst. Then, as long as you have acquired an abundant supply of healthy foods, this diet becomes effortless. Some people have never experienced natural thirst in their lives. From the moment in infancy when they were first given bottled milk with sugar, they became addicted. If you feel your natural thirst and hunger, suddenly natural and healthy foods become incredibly delicious. Everything you eat will begin tasting better.

14

—

THE POSITIVE RESPONSE TECHNIQUE

When we permit our hurt to hold us back from loving, we surrender our power to heal ourselves or to create meaningful change in our lives. Forgiving others for their mistakes as well as forgiving ourselves is essential to healing, so that love freely can flow again. Taking responsibility for healing ourselves and giving up overdependence on others opens the door to creating practical miracles.

Remembering the fact that our partner is different from us helps us to remember not to take things so personally. With this insight, we can accept their imperfections instead of being hurt by them. By practicing forgiveness, improving our communication skills, and asking for what we want, love can last for a lifetime. It is not enough just to change our attitude—practically everyone needs to learn new communication skills. Ideally, to get a marriage license, couples should be required to take both communication and parenting classes.

One of the easiest ways to release your hurt so that you can love freely is to take complete responsibility for your fulfillment. When your needs are not met by another, rather than hold on to hurt feelings, quickly change your focus. Don't dwell on your partner as the problem. Look to another need inside that has nothing to do with your partner. By shifting your focus and fulfilling another need inside, your new fulfillment will help you to focus on giving more to your partner instead of waiting for him or her to change.

By using the **Positive Response Technique,** you free yourself from the tendency to become hurt, offended, and defensive. When your partner doesn't fulfill your expectation, you will learn how to release your reactive tendencies to reject, withhold, and mistrust, and instead give yourself what you need to feel better.

In order to love as if for the first time, we must learn to heal our hurt. It is essential that we realize that we have the power to heal ourselves when we are hurt. Ultimately, what hurts us is forgetting we have that power, then becoming overly dependent on other people. Yes, they will disappoint, reject, and betray us, but it is our choice to forgive them and to learn never to expect perfection from them.

You are only hurting yourself by depending so much on others for perfection. It is fine to ask for what we want and to leave a relationship because we want more than it offers, but it is still a mistake to hold on to our feelings of anger and hurt and blame our partners. We should lovingly acknowledge our hurt, but then we need to learn from it so that we don't keep setting ourselves up for more pain. No one really causes our hurt. It is our unrealistic expectations or unloving demands that cause our hurt.

We should always lovingly acknowledge our hurt, but we must also be accountable for it.

To heal ourselves of hurt, we must first release the notion or belief that our partners are responsible for our feelings. Yes, they may hurt us or make us happy, but in the final analysis, it is we who become happy or pained. Our expectations for perfection make us hurt and our desire to give more makes us feel good. Ultimately, it is the act of giving that makes us happy. We are happy after receiving primarily because it motivates us to give freely.

When we can't give to our partners and instead feel hurt and self-pity, we need to recognize that we have become too dependent. We need to look to one of our other needs and fulfill it outside of the relationship. Most often, when we feel hurt in a relationship, the most important need we are missing is doing what we love and creating new experiences. To release our hurt, we need to give up whining and go out and do something on our own that is fun.

Release your self-pity by doing something on your own that makes you happy.

Before you can heal your hurt, you have to remove the cause. Overdependence on others—or on the opposite sex—to make us happy is almost always the culprit. Do something you would love to do on your own or with a friend and you easily will be able to let go of your hurt. If the hurt still lingers after you have taken this step, the Positive Response Technique will help you release it in just a few minutes.

Writing a Positive Response Letter

Even if everything you say about your partner when you are feeling mistrusting and resentful is accurate, it is still inappropriate to blame him or her for your inability to feel and respond with love. Whenever you are upset with your partner, take some time alone and ask yourself what he or she could say or do to make you feel better.

Write a letter to yourself as if it were from your partner expressing those very words and making the promises that you need to hear and depend on. If you need an apology, then write it out. Then ask yourself, if that happened, how would you feel? Next, write out your positive feelings of forgiveness, understanding, and gratitude in response.

By opening your heart in this way, you then can access your true self. Most of us can't, because while growing up the true self was not nurtured. A relationship can feel so good, because for at least some time, our partner's love and support awakens in us our willingness to love. Our true self emerges, and that is what makes us happy.

Ultimately, our goal is to stay connected always to our true self, but that is very rare and not necessary for a relationship to thrive. What is necessary is that we recognize when we are blocked from loving and realize that it is not our partner's fault. It is never his or her fault that we are not being loving. Our partner may make us feel angry or disturbed, but it is up to us to let go of our negative feelings and reawaken to our true self once again.

Mentally Creating a Positive Response

Another version of the Positive Response Technique is to rephrase in your mind what your partner is saying. Don't depend on him or her to speak your language; instead, learn his or her language, and then translate it. If your partner offends you with unsolicited advice, realize instead that he or she is really just trying to help the situation. Whatever your partner is doing is in some way an expression of caring and love.

Instead of rejecting love and demanding change, change your thinking and response. Recognize the attempt, and thank your partner for it. All you have to say is:

"Thanks for caring."

"Thanks for thinking about me."

"Thanks . . . that makes sense."

"Thanks . . . that's interesting. I would never have looked at it from that perspective."

By looking below the surface and appreciating another's positive intentions, we not only feel more loved, but also bestow on our partners the appreciation they deserve and enjoy.

In every distressing situation, think about what you would have wanted the person to say or do. Then, using your imagination, consider how that would have made you feel. While in touch with these feelings, respond with love, compassion, kindness, generosity, lightness, humor, sincerity, patience, or humility. When you are unassuming and less demanding, you will be much happier.

People often think or say, "If he (or she) was only nice to me, I would have been so generous."

This is a huge limitation. Don't let someone else's limitation and problems hold you back from being the magnanimous person you truly are. When others get to you and pull out your false-self reactions, be careful not to respond immediately. Take time to consider what you wanted, and after imagining that you got what you needed to have a loving and centered reaction, consider how you would have felt. This centered reaction is an expression of your true self. With this awareness of who you truly are, you can begin to consider how to respond wisely.

Sometimes, we resist feedback in relationships because we assume we have to do what our partner suggests for him or her to be happy. This is a mistake. People only remain demanding when they are not getting what they need. Generally, if your partner is offering advice, then what he or she needs from you is appreciation or understanding. Many times your partner just wants to be heard. If you realize that merely by listening you are giving a loving gift and thanking your partner for caring, he or she will not be so attached to your using the "good advice."

Pushing Away Feedback

Another reason we push away our partner's advice or support is that we incorrectly imagine they don't trust or care about us. While men often feel mistrusted, women feel uncared for if a man doesn't want to hear her.

Often a man really doesn't care about the details of a woman's day. What interests her just doesn't interest him. This does not mean he doesn't love her. What Carol said at a baby shower bores him. That's why he didn't go in the first place. This disinterest doesn't mean he doesn't care for his partner. If she were in danger, this same man would risk his life to save her, because he cares so much.

As long as the woman doesn't demand his interest, this caring man can learn to care more about the little things in her life. In addition, she can let him know how much she appreciates his attention even though he is not that interested. Although he is not fascinated by the details, he will be of help to her by being a caring partner to whom she can talk. A deeper understanding of what makes a woman happy helps a man to respect her basic needs and allows him to move gradually toward giving her more of what pleases her.

Likewise, as women learn more about men, they can and will begin giving more of what a man wants and enjoys most in a relationship. When a woman doesn't feel heard, she has a greater tendency to give a man lots of unsolicited advice, which can be very annoying. Instead of reacting negatively to this advice, he simply can remember that he doesn't have to do what she says and know that she is saying these things because she loves and cares for him.

The secret of success in relationships is not demanding change from our partner. It is fine to want it and ask for it, but it's not okay to demand it or use it to justify our pain and hurt. The winning philosophy in life is "to thine own self be true," then all else will be given unto you. Create changes in yourself so that you become the loving and positive person you truly are and you will get back the love and support you want.

Mental Rephrasing

Another way to use the Positive Response Technique is to rephrase in your mind whatever your partner says to you that is offensive or not supportive. Reflect on what was said and consider how you would have liked your partner to communicate his or her perspective more positively. Imagine it happened that way and explore how you would have reacted, then respond to the situation in a more centered and loving manner.

You cannot stop a reaction, but you can control how you respond to someone. Instead of responding based on your reactions, first question your reactions, transform negative reactions with the Positive Response Technique, and choose to respond with love and support. This way you are assured of getting more love in return.

By practicing the Positive Response Technique, you will

become more aware of what you want so that you more directly and calmly can ask for it. You also will realize how demanding and conditional your love is. By not taking things so personally, you can adjust to life and accept the limits and imperfections of others with greater love and forgiveness.

When this Positive Response Technique doesn't seem to work for you, it is clearly a sign of needing your partner too much. You need to shift gears by temporarily doing something else within your control that brings you fulfillment. With this in mind, try the Positive Response Technique again. If it still doesn't work, then move on to using the Blockbuster Technique in the following chapter.

15

THE BLOCKBUSTER
TECHNIQUE

When we enter into an intimate relationship, our biggest mistake is expecting and then depending too much on our partner's love. The secret to lasting love is creating an intimate relationship primarily for the purpose of giving, not getting. Ideally, before we marry, we should learn to be self-sufficient. When we already have a fulfilled life and love ourselves, we are not as dependent on our partner. If and when we get our partner's love, it is a special gift.

Instead of looking to our partner to give us the love we need, we need to look to ourselves, work, friends, groups, workshops, and therapy. It is a major mistake to look to our partner to fill us up. When we learn to give our love freely, without any demands on our partner, we are amazed to find how much more supportive she or he can be.

We cannot expect our partner to speak our language. If we want to be heard, we must gradually learn theirs. If we want more, we must first give up our demands for more and then ask for what we want in a tone and language they can understand. Reading *Men Are from Mars, Women Are from Venus* will free you to interpret your partner's messages correctly. **You will learn to give as if you already have what you need.**

Our inner blocks—resentment, depression, anxiety, and indifference—prevent us from acknowledging our true self and all the love in our hearts. By opening our hearts, we receive much more natural energy and keep passion alive, not just in romance, but in all areas of our life.

By using the **Blockbuster Process** you will be able to release twelve common blocks. In learning to identify and release them, you will be able to discharge emotional stress and distress most effectively. When you are upset, overwhelmed, nervous, or bored, you will have a practical tool for returning to feelings that are peaceful, happy, confident, or loving.

The Blockbuster Technique is an approach to dealing with negative feelings that allows you to heal without suppressing or inflicting negativity on others. It frees you to take 100 percent responsibility for resolving your inner issues. Regardless of what unpleasant or negative feeling you may have inside, you will gain the power to remove it. This technique can be done by writing in a journal or by discharging. Sometimes when discharging doesn't work, writing out the feelings explored in this technique will allow you to experience miraculous results.

In all of my books, I have developed and taught earlier stages and versions of this technique, naming it the Love Letter Technique Technique, the Emotional Release Technique, the Forgiveness Letter Technique, the Feeling Letter Technique, and the Feeling Better Technique. Each of these worked and still does. The Blockbuster Technique is just a more precise and streamlined version. It is, however, more complicated. You may wish to begin by simply using the Feeling Better Technique, which served me well for fifteen years.

The Feeling Better Technique is all most people need to do to start seeing their blocks begin to disappear. This specific process helps us to release blame by directing our attention in such a way that we more easily can feel and let go of our underlying emotions.

When we are stuck in one feeling or state, by simply acknowledging and experiencing deeper underlying feelings and emotions we give ourselves the nurturing we need, and the block is easily released. Instead of being stuck, we are free to choose our response from a loving, adult perspective.

Whenever we are upset and want to feel better, by just taking some time to write out and listen to our feelings of anger, sadness, fear, and sorrow, we can begin to feel better again. Let's first explore the Feeling Better Technique.

Writing a Feeling Better Letter

To process, heal, and let go of negative feelings, rather than sharing these feelings with the person with whom we are upset, write out a mock letter. Pretend you are sharing all your feelings with the person who has upset you and that he or she is listening. Take a few minutes to move through each of the levels of a Feeling Better Letter. Here is a helpful format to follow:

> Dear_____,
>   I am angry [*frustrated or annoyed*] that . . .
>   I am sad [*disappointed or hurt*] that . . .
>   I am afraid [*worried or scared*] that . . .
>   I am sorry [*embarrassed or ashamed*] that . . .
>   I understand [*forgive, know, trust, and thank
>   you for*] . . .
>   I love you,

Saying "I love you" at the end of the letter is very cathartic. If the person to whom you are writing is not intimate with you, then simply end the letter with "Sincerely yours."

The next time you are upset and want to feel better, then write a Feeling Better Letter. Sometimes it only takes ten minutes to cool off, while at other times it may take longer.

When you feel you must "have a talk" with a person, or tell him or her off, or teach someone a lesson, then clearly you are looking in the wrong direction. Not only will you be abusive, but you also will not feel any better yourself. When you are upset at someone, even if it is your intimate partner, don't expect him or her to be sympathetic to your emotional turmoil while he or she feels attacked by blame.

Instead, write a Feeling Better Letter. Once you return to being more loving and forgiving, then, if it is still necessary, you can approach your partner with friendly feedback or simply communicate what you would like in the future.

Sometimes after writing a Feeling Better Letter, if you still don't feel a rush of forgiveness, compose a short response letter. In this letter, say to yourself all of the things you would want this person to say to you. After writing out the apologies and putting on paper what you need to hear, you are able to experience forgiveness.

Ideally, when parents apologize for their mistakes and overreactions, children learn to forgive. It is easy for a child to forgive his or her parents. Unless the parent apologizes, the child blames himself or herself and not only can't forgive others, but develops low self-esteem. Writing the Feeling Better Letter and then a response letter helps to teach us how to forgive more freely.

Using the Blockbuster Chart

The Blockbuster Technique is based on a chart used to navigate through the murky waters of feelings. Often we become stuck in life and don't know how to move on. This chart helps shed some light on what emotions we may be missing that need to be felt as well as what positive feelings we need to express.

I remember twenty years ago being stuck all night in an airport in Japan during wintertime, and the airport was freezing. I was on my way to the Philippines to teach a seminar. The airport kept opening and closing. Our flight was on and off all night long. This was on top of an already lengthy twelve-hour journey. I was tired and pushed beyond my limits. I literally felt like killing someone. Then, an event occurred that removed all my anguish.

I remember several times finding enormous relief when someone would come on the loudspeaker and say, "We understand your inconvenience; we are doing everything we can. Thank you for your patience." Each time they said "Thank you for your patience," I suddenly felt incredible relief. I just needed someone to remind me of what I needed to feel in that moment. I should have been practicing patience, but instead was caught thinking I had to be outraged by this bad treatment.

This Blockbuster Chart reveals the twelve most common blocks and helps you to identify the positive qualities of the self that are being blocked. Many times people don't even recognize their blocks until they begin to look at what positive qualities they are missing. Let's review the Blockbuster Chart and some ways to use it:

The Blockbuster Chart

BLOCK	FEELING	EMOTION	TRUE SELF
1. Resentment	Deprived	Angry	Peace
2. Depression	Abandoned	Sad	Joy
3. Confusion	Hopeless	Afraid	Confidence
4. Indifference	Inadequate	Sorry	Love
5. Judgments	Dissatisfied	Frustrated	Patience
6. Procrastination	Discouraged	Disappointed	Optimism
7. Indecision	Powerless	Worried	Strength
8. Perfectionism	Humiliated	Embarrassed	Humility
9. Jealousy	Insulted	Furious	Fulfillment
10. Self-pity	Betrayed	Hurt	Inspiration
11. Anxiety	Helpless	Scared	Courage
12. Guilt	Unworthy	Ashamed	Innocence

There are four steps to using this chart:

1. If you want to feel more of a true-self quality, then identify the block that is holding you back. For example, if you don't feel peace, your block is resentment. If you don't feel joy, your block is depression, and so on.

2. To overcome this block, write a Feeling Better Letter using the feelings and emotions linked to your block, including the next three levels down the chart. For example, if your block is resentment, then explore these feelings:
   - Deprivation and anger
   - Abandonment and sadness
   - Hopelessness and fear
   - Inadequacy and sorrow

3. By exploring and expressing your wants, needs, or wishes, you immediately will begin to release the block. Focus more on how you want to be or feel rather than on how you want others to change.

4. Then feel better by exploring and expressing such positive feelings as understanding, appreciation, trust, and forgiveness.

What makes this chart work is the basic idea that having greater awareness of what you are feeling inside always will make you feel better. This is not a mere concept; as you use this chart, it will become very practical.

If you are stuck in negative feelings, then look for them on the chart. To remove your block associated with these feelings, use the Blockbuster Technique and either write out your feelings or directly discharge them.

All this is quickly determined by looking at the chart. For each of the twelve blocks, there is a different route to free ourselves of the issues that may be new or may have held us back our whole lives. Each of these blocks is explored more fully in chapters 16 and 17 of my book *How to Get What You Want and Want What You Have.*

16

—

THE ATTITUDE
ADJUSTMENT TECHNIQUE

When we work primarily for the money, it is more difficult to feel our true needs or appreciate what we have now. When we are already happy, we don't feel an urgent need for money to make us happier. The real truth is that we always have exactly what we need to take our next step in our life's journey.

With a clearer awareness of what we really need, we more easily can stay balanced and not be swayed by the temptations of greater success. We learn that by prioritizing what is really important, we can have plenty of money and also be happy, healthy, and in love.

When we suffer or feel stressed, it is because we are not recognizing that in this moment we always have everything we need to be happy. Without a clear awareness of our different needs and how to fulfill each one, we cannot appreciate or benefit from what we have now. When you are not so dependent on money to make you happy, you are free to create whatever you want, including more money. That is what work as if money doesn't matter is all about.

Discover your power to create miraculous results and literally design your daily destiny with the **Attitude Adjustment Technique**. Although you cannot always control events, you can control your attitude and feelings about them. By learning to generate a positive attitude during the day, you will become a magnet attracting the success you have planned. By increasing your focus on improving the quality of your daily experience, you will not only stay connected to your true self, but you will also experience greater rewards in the outer world.

After spending a few minutes recharging or discharging, take a few minutes to organize your day. Think about the things you expect to happen. If you don't have many expectations, then just reflect on how you want your day to unfold. If you have expectations, think about them, and then reflect on how you want your day to unfold.

This planning needs to be within very realistic limits. Although it is sometimes good to think freely of all the things you want to happen, that is not this technique. To plan from your heart, start in your head. Think about what is reasonable to expect. Be very reasonable.

Next, imagine things happening a little bit better—not a whole lot better, but just a little better, so that it is still fairly reasonable. Making this adjustment is the beginning step of changing your attitude. Don't push too far if it is not reasonable. Now you are imagining a good or better day.

Next, take a leap, and based on your most positive past experiences, imagine the best happening. Within the realm of reason, imagine having a great day, or at least feeling great even though things are not perfect. If someone always annoys you and you can't realistically imagine them changing, then imagine being able to be around them without feeling so annoyed.

As you imagine the best happening, then imagine how that would make you feel.

The exploration of these positive feelings will assist you in making a shift back to your true and positive self. Use these phrases to draw out these positive feelings:

Right now I am happy that . . .

Right now I am confident that . . .

Right now I am so grateful for . . .

Next, come back into present time and give thanks for your many blessings. By doing this technique for a few minutes, you will be refreshed and ready to create the best day possible. Although we cannot always determine what others say and do, we can determine our own attitude.

By taking a few minutes to adjust our attitude, a door opens for the day to be different. When we change, the world changes too. You will see that, as you imagine feeling more positive during the day, more positive things start to happen.

This technique is explored in greater detail in my book *How to Get What You Want and Want What You Have* and is called "Setting Your Intention." These instructions provide enough direction for you to begin.

17

THE WILLFUL BREATHING TECHNIQUE

No one has a perfect, problem-free existence. To relax fully, you must accept your life and its unique challenges. Make a lemon into lemonade or sometimes ignore the lemon and drink orange juice. Better yet, enjoy a glass of plain water. From this place of acceptance, go on passionately to desire more.

To get what you want, first appreciate what you have. It is only when we are relaxed and open that we can begin to recognize the endless possibilities that always exist to create positive and meaningful change. With this vision of positive possibilities, we can appreciate our true desires and not be led astray by addictive tendencies and cravings. Whenever we are acting out of fear and worry, we are missing the whole picture. When you feel anxious, worried, afraid, or helpless, it is always best to postpone making any lasting decisions if possible. When we feel that way in a relation-

ship, we need to postpone a discussion and then shift gears
to doing something that doesn't create fear.

We can breathe easily when we begin to acknowledge we
already have what we need. By combining some easy-to-use
Willful Breathing Techniques with decharging, you immediately can link up with the mind-body connection that is
essential for health, peak athletic performance, endurance,
sexual appetite, and effortless weight loss, as well as
improved job performance and stamina. **You will be able to
relax as if everything will be okay.**

This technique was described in chapter 11 (page 166) as
a preparation for recharging. It simply involves breathing a
little deeper than usual in response to your willful intention.
By simply thinking, "Breathe in" and then "Breathe out,"
the connection between your conscious will and your body
is strengthened.

Whenever your body is not cooperating with your intention, this technique will do wonders. For example, when
your body will not burn unwanted fat, simply do this technique. So often exercise is recommended to lose weight.
When exercise is effective, one of the reasons it works is that
you are forced to apply your will against your body's resistance to exercise.

This is the old way of losing weight. It is like saying that
you have to force yourself to do something you don't want
to do in order to lose weight. It is no wonder that so many
overweight people stop going to the gym. Instead of pushing
so hard, by simply doing willful breathing for ten or twenty
minutes a day (or even three times a week), you will get
many of the same healthy results that come from regular
exercise.

Once you have lost the extra weight and you are in harmony and connected with your body, you naturally will
want to exercise. **Exercise is a luxury of the fit and not the
best way to lose weight.** Until you've achieved your desired

weight, don't exercise unless you want to. Instead, use your breath to connect you to your body and generate better health.

There are two ways to do this technique. Start out by sitting down and doing it so that it becomes easy to do. Once you know the steps, go for a walk and do it. In this case you will find that the walking makes willful breathing much easier. As you walk, the body naturally wants to do your will and breathe in and out a little deeper than usual.

The secret of willful breathing is to make sure that you are not pushing yourself too hard. While walking, keep your pace to a point where you are not out of breath and thus have to huff and puff or breathe through your mouth. If you are congested and can't breathe in through your nose, then sense the point at which you would have to breathe through your mouth if you were less congested.

People who are sick or recovering can get many of the benefits of exercise by sitting and doing this technique or by going for short walks. For convalescents, it is done more easily in a group or privately with the help of a nurse. This simply means not doing it alone but having someone also doing it in the same room. More people doing it together and in sync makes it much easier.

When you push so hard that you have to breathe in through your mouth, then your body is producing lactic acid. Instead of helping your body, you are generating toxins. By staying at this limit, breathing in through your nose, you will restore your body's ability to heal itself and awaken its ability to burn fat without having to exhaust yourself. You can exhale through your nose or mouth. There is no longer any need to struggle with exercise and then eventually give up and feel guilty. Give up the guilt, and breathe a sigh of relief.

18

NATURAL ENERGY HEALING

The first requirement for healing and success is learning to feel natural energy. When you ask for more of this energy, the empowerment that results assures you that you are being heard. You cannot see the wind, but you know it exists, because you can feel it and understand its influence. Likewise, you cannot see natural energy, but you can know it is listening by its immediate response to your requests.

For those seeking to know God or a spiritual reality, recharging, discharging, and Natural Energy Healing confirms there is a God. When you feel God's energy flow to you in response to your request, then God and the support God provides are no longer concepts to be debated and questioned, but a direct experience. The proof is in the pudding. When you can feel God's energy immediately respond to your requests, then you know God is there for you. **Then you can talk to God as if you are being heard.**

By practicing **Natural Energy Healing** you will learn to heal others and receive healing from them. You will begin to experience new levels of confidence in your miraculous power. By healing others, you receive the rare opportunity to know clearly that natural energy or God's magnificent power is working through you. You can use this increased energy to create miracles in your work and relationships as well.

One does not have to be a professional healer to have this empowering experience. By simply practicing on friends and family members, this power can grow. Many people simply volunteer at their local church, support group, or hospital to do occasional healings. Many massage therapists, chiropractors, acupuncturists, doctors, nurses, dentists, and medical assistants have added natural energy healing into their assortment of powerful tools to assist the healing of their clients and patients.

Stage 1: Activation

The technique of Natural Energy Healing will be described and discussed more fully in a later book entitled *The Search for Healing Power*. The first stage of this simple healing process easily can be practiced once you can feel the energy during recharging and decharging. In this stage, you are activating the healing power in your client. You are simply starting up their car by recharging their self-healing batteries.

While healing someone, raise your hands in the air and say ten times, either silently or aloud, your recharging memorized intention (MI). When you feel the energy flowing, then simply ask Natural Healing Energy to use you to heal this person.

First begin by turning on your fingertips with ten repetitions of your basic recharge MI. Once you feel the energy flowing, then say:

Healing Energy,
I really need your help.
Please come.
Use me to heal this person.
Awaken in this person your healing power.
Thank you.

My favorite position is to stand behind the person being healed while they are sitting comfortably in a chair. Once I have said this MI out loud, then I easily and effortlessly continue to repeat it silently, as I slowly move my fingertips to touch their forehead. It is a simple move.

Imagine a line from the top of their nose across the forehead. From behind, I lightly press my ten fingers on their forehead along that line. This spot tends to be a very receptive spot to send healing energy.

As you mentally repeat your healing MI, ask the person being healed to take ten deep breaths. As he or she does this, you will find that the energy increases in flow. You may then wish to increase the flow with deeper breathing as well. Do what creates a greater flow.

If they commonly talk to God, then ask them to pray out loud to God so that you can hear. Sometimes, as they put into words what they are feeling and wanting, the energy flow increases. If they don't feel comfortable talking to God, then simply have them express out loud their feelings, wants, needs, intentions, and wishes. You can have them use these following lead-in phrases to awaken their feelings:

"This sickness makes me feel . . . "

"Right now I am wanting . . . "

"Right now in my life I really, really need . . . "

"If I were healthy I would . . . "

"I wish . . . "

By expressing these different feelings, either to God in a prayer or simply sharing with you as you silently continue repeating your healing MI, they will in effect be opening themselves up to receive more healing energy. When you notice more energy start flowing, let them know. This is important feedback for them to know what vulnerable attitudes open the door for more healing energy to come in.

Using this technique, I started out feeling little bits of energy, but within weeks it started to increase. Instead of just feeling relaxing peace, which is a good gift to give someone, people started to feel the healing energy, and sometimes their symptoms lessened or went away in one session. In the first three or four minutes of a session, one should not expect a transmission of energy. Instead, expect a buzzing of energy in your fingers and an awakening or buzzing of energy in the client.

Stage 2: Discharging a Sickness or Condition

After this "awakening" or "activation" of the self-healing energy, the next stage of healing is to discharge a person. This should not be attempted until you have learned to discharge. To discharge a sickness, use this discharging MI:

Healing Energy,
I really need your help.
Please come.
Use me to discharge this person.
Use these hands to draw out their excess energy.
Thank you.

When discharging someone, place the fingers of your left hand on their forehead and the fingers of your right hand comfortably at the back of their neck. Exact placement is not necessary. You may also hold both hands near and surrounding a wounded or sick part of the body.

Stage 3: Recharging After the Decharge

Once the stuck excess energy has been drawn out, then the person is ready to receive a fresh flow of natural or divine energy through your hands. This transmission of energy recharges the body, mind, heart, and spirit with healing energy.

To recharge your client or patient, use this recharging MI:

Healing Energy,
I really need your help.
Thank you for coming.
Use me to recharge this person.
Right now, through my hands, send your healing
energy.
Thank you.

There are many more advanced healing techniques, but these three levels are an important beginning. Make sure that when you heal it is not out of a sense of obligation, but coming from a place of joy or pleasure. If you feel burdened by the responsibility in any way, then it will not work. In doing this natural energy technique it is not necessary to spend more than ten minutes. Take about a minute to turn on your fingertips and about three minutes for each of the three stages. You could do it as a gift every day for someone or once a week. By following these guidelines, you will be able to begin one of the most fulfilling journeys I ever have experienced.

After healing a person or many persons, always take fifteen minutes to decharge excess energy you may have absorbed, and then recharge. Ten minutes of decharging and five minutes to recharge is generally enough. Never be afraid of absorbing a person's sickness. If you can take it in, then you can easily send it out. The tendency to absorb a sickness is minimal, particularly because you are not absorbing the sickness, but the excess energy. Then, after decharging a person, you send the energy back into them to recharge them. As long as you feel the tingling energy in your fingertips, the movement of energy from the patient or client is self-purifying.

It is also important to note that you are not intending to absorb their excess energy in your body. While decharging, simply feel the energy flow to your fingertips and then out into the space around you. Don't intend to pull it into your body. Remember, you are asking "healing energy" to do the job. You don't have to do anything but keep intending and let "healing energy" do the work.

Self-healing

To heal yourself directly, use the different natural elements to assist you. These are some examples:

Stage 1 Self-healing: Activation

Healing Energy,
I really need your help.
Please come.
Use this rose to heal my condition.
Awaken in me your healing power.
Thank you.

Stage 2 Self-healing: Decharging a Sickness or Condition

Healing Energy,
I really need your help.
Please come.
Use this rose to decharge my condition.
Use this rose to draw out my excess energy.
Thank you.

Stage 3 Self-healing: Recharging

Healing Energy,
I really need your help.
Thank you for coming.
Use this rose to recharge me.
Right now, through this rose, send me your healing
energy.
Thank you.

In this way, you can use any of the natural elements to assist you in self-healing any emotional block or physical pain and sickness.

19

THE "WHAT IF" TECHNIQUE

To tap into your power to create miracles, it is most important that you give yourself permission to want more and enjoy. Give yourself permission to explore all your wants. You must feast as if you have unlimited possibilities. Take risks, do what you want, and then learn if that is what you really want. Don't trust me or anyone else. Find out for yourself what is true and right for you.

This is most concretely experienced by practicing the Natural Energy Diet. By making a few significant differences, you will be free to feel your true desires for the foods that are most healthy for you. In this way, without feeling in any way that you are giving up something, a door opens and you begin to feel that there is an abundance of delicious foods for you to eat.

Every moment is always presenting us with millions of

opportunities to get what we need. By releasing our fixation and addiction to unhealthy foods, we literally enjoy and want more healthy food. This is true in all areas of life. Instead of getting caught up in a blindness of limited possibilities, with a little practice we can begin opening our eyes to the limitless possibilities that exist for us.

By practicing the **"What If" Exercise** you will experience who you are without all the imagined limitations we put on ourselves. By simply exploring your responses to a series of "what if" questions, you are then freer to find your true self. With a little practice, you will begin to see that in every area of your life there are limitless possibilities for you to lead a happy, healthy, rich, and fulfilled life.

When you put into practice each of these nine important principles and try out these new natural energy tools and self-healing techniques, you instantly will experience your power to forge the life you desire. Mastery of any of these tools is not required to see immediate results. But once you learn to recharge and decharge, all the doors automatically will begin to open.

When business, life, or your partner disturbs you, rather than staying disturbed, you can learn to change your state by simply using the "What If" Technique. One way to do this is by asking yourself, "What if they were to apologize or say something really nice to me or make it up to me in some way? How would I feel then?" By exploring this possibility, you are then back to feeling a heartfelt, true response. Whenever you feel good or forgiving, you are in touch with your true self.

Instead of being limited by the actions of others or the circumstances of your past, by simply asking, "What if . . . ?" and then imagining how you would feel if circumstances were more supportive, you immediately can become more connected to your true self. By making this change within yourself, you will become more open and flexible, and then the world around you will become more open and accepting of you.

Many people complain that they didn't get the support they needed in childhood. Rather than remain victims of our past, we can change the influence of our personal history to support us rather than hold us back. To be free of the limiting aspects of the past, we must first understand how our past can support us. A negative experience cannot be removed directly, but it can be replaced with a positive one.

When we were children, if we were loved, we developed the knowledge that we are lovable. This provides the basis for increased confidence, self-forgiveness, and other fine qualities. This ability to love ourselves is already within ourselves, but it is triggered by our parents' nurturing support. If we didn't get that support at a young age, then we end up making a lot of choices in life without this vital insight.

Later in life, by exploring "What if we did get the support we missed," we are, actually, undoing the effects of the past. By exploring "what if," we give ourselves the option to trigger and awaken our feelings of self-love. By connecting to our true selves, which were suppressed in the past, we are then able to use our past to support us.

Let's say that you have difficulty forgiving others. By going back and remembering mistakes your parents made and asking yourself, "What if they apologized and corrected their behavior?" you will begin to feel increasing forgiveness for them. With this ability to forgive them, you will find it much easier to forgive others and yourself in present time. It can be very useful to look at our pasts and remember past pain when we are doing it in the context of using those memories to feel better and not worse.

Once you have posed a "What if?" question, ask more questions to draw out your feelings. Following are a few examples of follow-up questions.

Ask yourself, "What if I had all the money in the world?" Then ask other questions like:

"What would I do?"

"How would I feel?"

"How would I be reacting right now?"

"What would I choose to do?"

"How would I feel about myself?"

"How would I feel about my future?"

"How would I feel about my boss?"

"How would I treat my spouse?"

More examples of "What if" questions to ask yourself are:

"What if I were single again?"

"What if I had no fear?"

"What if I were happily married?"

"What if I were healthy?"

"What if I had only one more year to live?"

"What if I knew that I had as many lives to live as I wanted?"

"What if I weren't addicted to sugar; what would I want to eat?"

"What if I had more time; what would I do?"

"What if I were more educated?"

"What if I were getting everything I needed in my marriage; how would I treat my spouse today?"

In this exercise, you don't have to be reasonable—just let yourself be free to imagine "What if?" This is the basis of all of the nine guiding principles.

1. What if you could learn to create miracles? What would you do?

2. What if you were free to do what you wanted? What choices would you make?

3. What if you were an innocent beginner? What questions would you ask? How would you feel toward others and education?

4. What if you were giving love for the first time? How would you love and share your heart?

5. What if you had everything you needed? How would you react to your partner?

6. What if money really didn't matter? What work would you do? What business decisions would you make?

7. What if you could relax because you knew that everything always turns out okay? What would you choose to do to make sure that happened?

8. What if you knew God or a higher power, a guardian angel or whatever, was listening and was willing to help you? How would you pray and how often?

9. What if you could eat whatever you want because you are not addicted to unhealthy food or situations? How would you feel and what would you do differently?

While doing the "What If" Exercise, don't be concerned about whether something is possible or even reasonable. Just let yourself feast on exploring what you want and then imagine how you would feel getting it. So much of the time, we don't allow ourselves to imagine having or wanting more. Our mind sets up conditions that block the free and open flow of our desires. As you learn to connect with your random desires, you gradually come closer to discovering your soul's desires.

By exploring your desire, you may at first feel that you want to quit your job, but as you continue to explore your many wants, you may find that you want to enjoy your job more and get more respect. Eventually, you may begin to feel that you want to do your best and be an example to inspire others how to behave in a challenging situation.

Desire is like a river that when blocked becomes stale and murky. But by letting go in the freedom of considering infinite possibilities of what is in the river of desire, the stream begins to flow and automatically begins to purify itself. Let your hidden desires come out in the sunshine of your consciousness and they automatically will become more aligned with your divine nature. You then will experience the peace, joy, confidence, and love that come from feeling your soul desires.

20

THE POWER IS ALREADY
WITHIN YOU

The miraculous healing and success that any person can now experience comes from developing our own inner ability to create practical miracles. This power is already within everyone. Our bodies and brains are wired to access and express it. All we have to do is awaken it. **The nine guiding principles and techniques for creating miracles will do just that.** With a few minor adjustments you easily will be able to put them into practice.

The capacity to comprehend and apply these principles has been growing in our consciousness for the last two thousand years and more clearly in the last two hundred years. They are not new ideas, but they are arranged and expressed in a new way. Together they function as a lens to bring into sharper focus the most important spiritual issues mankind has struggled to understand and follow throughout recent history. In our brighter moments, these are the underlying principles by which people of all backgrounds aspire to live their lives.

By updating and integrating your understanding of these principles with your own personal experience and common sense, things you dreamed of but couldn't strive for become attainable and practical reality. This book is not in any way intended to persuade you, but rather to awaken, validate, or articulate what you already know to be true but have not put fully into practice yet.

Life Can Be Easier

Life becomes so much easier when you learn to create practical miracles. Toil and suffering or ease and comfort—the choice is now yours. In the past we didn't have that choice. Only a few people possessed the capacity to awaken and use their miraculous potential, but now it is universal.

Even if you are with the right person, working in the right job, or following the right diet, success can be difficult to achieve unless you apply each of the nine principles. Some people do manage to achieve success without using all nine, but their lives are sometimes filled with pain. These nine techniques when needed can generate immediate and miraculous results.

There are infinite ways to improve the mind, body, heart, and spirit. Personal growth can be very simple. It is like cooking a meal. All it takes to make a great meal is food, water, and heat. These are constants. The permutations and combinations of ways to make a delicious meal are endless. And yet, even if you create the perfect dinner for you, there is no guarantee that everyone else will like it. Any cook knows there is no one recipe that appeals to everyone.

**To define one approach as the only approach is like
saying there is only one way to make dinner.**

This book is my meal, cooked for you. Though the words may not be correct for everyone, I hope many of them are for you. At worst, I think it can provide you with helpful insight. At best, it is a perfect fit and works right away. Within days or weeks you will begin creating practical miracles.

Please don't be put off if you don't relate to some of my ideas or if they seem too far out or impossible. I agree that they were impossible for most people to put into practice in the past. That is why they feel like miracles.

Just because one idea doesn't work for you doesn't mean others are not valid. We are all human and prone to making mistakes. I am doing my best to find the right words for as many people as possible to understand. I hope you wisely will pick and choose what works for you and keep an open mind long enough to test many of these principles and practices.

Practice and Believing

You can create miracles, but it takes practice and belief. This is generally an easier task for younger people. The older we become, the more conditioned we are by our past experience. We know what we can do and what we can't. If I failed at singing or writing, then I assume I am not good at those things. Yet sometimes our greatest or most painful disappointments in life have to do with our greatest gifts.

When I was a young teenager, my greatest fear was public speaking. I gave my first lecture on meditation and developing your full mental potential at the age of nineteen. I was so nervous and just plain scared that my knees began to shake involuntarily. Then, as I faced my audience with a completely blank mind, I fainted. People thought I had died.

If I had given up public speaking then and there, I would never have developed one of my greatest gifts. It now takes no effort for me to give talks before an audience of thousands. It is one of my greatest pleasures in life and a source of tremendous inspiration for both my audience and for me. There is no longer even a hint of anxiety or fear.

Our greatest fears often cover up our greatest talents or gifts in life.

It took me ten years to overcome all my anxieties and realize my hidden gift. Having developed my speaking abilities, I kept feeling the urge to write a book. Yet I also felt stuck. In school, writing was my weakest subject while math was my strongest. I simply wasn't a good writer, and I experienced enormous frustration just trying. During college, it would take me hours and days to write a few pages. I could not believe how easy writing was for my friends. Clearly, writing was not for me.

Now I have written twelve bestsellers and tend to be a speed writer. At the beginning of my writing career, it took several years to put my ideas down in an organized and coherent fashion. Now, after many years of developing my thoughts, it takes me only a few months to write them down and create a book. What used to be an arduous task has become one of my greatest strengths and pleasures.

For years as a healer I could not feel the healing energy as I do now. It was not until about three years ago that I was able to dramatically accelerate a person's self-healing ability even with life-threatening diseases. This most recent shift was not from a lot of hard work, but because the consciousness in the world has changed. Not only can I feel and direct this miraculous healing energy, but most everyone in my workshops can as well. You just need someone to point out the energy and teach you how to use it.

Most of these workshop participants are amazed because they were not aware of any change in their abilities. Yet, suddenly they are able to begin feeling and accumulating subtle natural energy. They experience the benefits right away. Until they had an opportunity to learn something new, they never knew they possessed the hidden abilities that are now suddenly available to them.

The Limits of Religion

The shift that has just occurred has been evolving slowly for thousands of years. Jesus, who is famous for demonstrating miracles, said, "I have not come to answer your questions; instead, I come to show you what you will become."

He could not teach others this mastery, as they were not ready, but he could inspire them and give them hope. He said, "I speak in stories or parables because you cannot understand, but one day you will." It is only now that people are capable of comprehending the spiritual truths required to create miracles.

The great teacher and miracle worker Buddha shared the same vision. He said there were certain questions that he could not answer because the people were not yet ready. He knew that if he tried, they just wouldn't and couldn't understand. The best he could do was to teach an appropriate message for the people of his time to help alleviate suffering. He, like Jesus, faced the wall that every teacher confronts. You can only teach what the student is ready to hear and understand.

**No matter how much you know, you can only teach
what the student is ready to hear and understand.**

We are fortunate to be living at a time when most people
are ready to comprehend and put into practice that which in
the past could be known only to a few. In very real terms, all
of us are now equal in our ability to access our inner potential to create practical miracles and make our dreams come
true. All that people need is the necessary education to
awaken their inner power, and that is now available in an
unlimited supply.

People of all religions and spiritual inclinations will have
the potential to strike up a conversation while waiting in the
checkout line of their favorite grocery store and feel they are
talking to a wonderful spiritual being, regardless of their religion. Religious prejudice, which has been and still is responsible for extraordinary violence and mistrust, will be released. In
this age of miracles, a seeker of transformation, change, and
spiritual attainment is not offended when another's spiritual
approach is different from his or her own.

I remember a woman in one of my seminars sharing this
simple but delightful truth. "I was doing one of the exercises
with a Hindu person," she said. "I am a born-again Christian and always mistrusted people who did not believe in
Jesus. When I got to know the Hindu man, I realized he was
just as good a person as I am and very spiritual. This experience helped me to open my mind and recognize the good in
all people and all faiths."

From that positive occurrence, she experienced the shift
that is the foundation of America and any other free democracy: religious freedom, real tolerance with the heartfelt
recognition that there is no one way for everyone. Though
this was the vision of the founding fathers and mothers of

America, we are still struggling to achieve it. Even the word "tolerance," which essentially means to embrace and accept differences, comes with a negative connotation. For many people, tolerance has meant putting up with the differences or allowing them to exist while secretly judging others' ways to be inferior to their own.

Giving Up "One Way" Thinking

Children are the best examples of "one way" thinking. When a child doesn't have access to the knowledge of the world, he or she rightly needs and depends on his or her parents for guidance. To feel secure, children need to believe they are following the right leader. As a result, every young child thinks his or her parents are the best and that their way is the best way.

As children reach about nine years old, a change in the brain occurs, and they suddenly see themselves, the world, and their parents differently. Self-awareness increases, and they begin to feel embarrassed by their parents. Suddenly, singing in public or talking about them is not allowed.

Next, around age thirteen or fourteen, another stage of brain development occurs. Our cherished parental status as infinitely brilliant and wise is reduced to ashes. Teenagers suddenly think they know everything, and we know nothing. This movement through adolescence, which every parent has experienced, helps us to understand the evolution of mankind.

Teenagers suddenly think they know everything and their parents know nothing.

The gradual separation of church and state, followed by the eventual development of scientific thinking, reflects the same changes we see in growing children. Separation of church and state could occur when the consciousness of mankind became able to think for itself. Like a nine-year-old embarrassed by his or her parents' perceived inadequacies, mankind realized that the church was not perfect and that, therefore, they would do better to rule themselves.

The movement toward science occurred when this change was complete. Mankind realized that divine authority was misleading and that any person had just as much potential to know what was right as the church. Everyone had the ability to know what was true. It was from this point that the whole notion of scientific research and inquiry evolved.

Like teenagers rejecting the omnipotence and omniscience of their parents, many followers of the new religion of science rejected the old religious traditions as complete ignorance, while arrogantly proclaiming the superiority of scientific research. As we were free to follow a path of reason, we then could freely open our hearts to experiment more.

This was expressed historically through the Renaissance and other times of cultural and artistic acceleration in society. With each generation, there was new art and new music, and we continued to break free of one-way thinking. This was the beginning of the notion of freedom and equality.

Then came the birth of democracy, when people would no longer be ruled by just the mind or heart. We wanted the freedom to choose and do what we felt was good and just within ourselves. This evolutionary development is responsible for the expansion of democracy in the last two hundred years.

The Blessings of This New Age

Now, as we move into this millennium, our new challenge is not only still to follow our minds and hearts but also to follow our consciences in the process of doing our duty and making our dreams come true. This is an exciting challenge and journey. By following the nine guiding principles and using the different techniques, you will have much of the support you need. I hope you pack this book with you on your trip and use it to help support you, your friends, and your family.

Let it guide you, or simply remind you to come back, come back to the miraculous power and truth that has been waiting within you to emerge. Use this book to help you remember who you really are and what you are here to do. Use it to remember that you are not alone and that you were never alone. Use it to remember that you are much bigger than you were before. Use it to remember that you are free.

Exercise your new freedom by choosing to be more and do more. You have a new power to change your life and create, with God's help and the help of those who love you, the life you have always wanted.

May your heart be filled right now and forever with God's blessings of peace, joy, confidence, and love. May your mind be open right now and forever to God's blessings of patience, optimism, strength, and humility. May your life be touched right now and forever by God's blessings of fulfillment, inspiration, courage, and innocence. May you always and forever give thanks to God for the many blessings you have received and will continue receive.

I give thanks to God for blessing me with the opportunity to write this book, and I thank you once again for letting me be a part of your journey in this world. May you always be free to share your love and light in whatever way you choose at this most beautiful and wondrous time to be alive. May God and all God's angels bless you always and be by your side as you walk into radiant sunshine of this glorious new age.

How to locate a Mars Venus Counselling Centre in the United Kingdom licensed by John Gray:

Website	www.mars-venus.co.uk
Email	enquiries@mars-venus.co.uk
Telephone	+44(0)1536 743 997
Fax	+44(0)1536 460 441
Mail	PO Box 6158, NN18 8ZB

Other John Gray books available from Vermilion

Mars and Venus Together Forever	0 09 181489 8	£7.99
Mars and Venus in the Bedroom	0 09 181529 0	£7.99
Mars and Venus on a Date	0 09 181552 5	£7.99
Mars and Venus in Love	0 09 181524 X	£7.99
What Your Mother Couldn't Tell You and Your Father Didn't Know	0 09 180653 4	£9.99
Mars and Venus Starting Over	0 09 181627 0	£7.99
Mars and Venus 365 Ways to Keep Your Love Alive	0 09 181696 3	£1.99
Men Are From Mars, Women Are From Venus Book of Days	0 09 182710 8	£5.99
Men Are From Mars, Women Are From Venus, Children Are From Heaven	0 09 182616 0	£7.99
How To Get What You Want and Want What You Have	0 09 185126 2	£6.99

To order copies of any of these books direct from Vermilion (p&p free), call the TBS Direct credit-card hotline on 01621 819 596.

Vermilion books are also available from all good booksellers.